IF I CAN SURVIVE, YOU CAN TOO....

A STORY OF CONQUERING NEAR DEATH SITUATION IN LIFE...

BIJOY ANANDA LANGTHASA

Made with ❤ on the Notion Press Platform
www.notionpress.com

I dedicate this book to my mother.

When I close my eyes and think about this book, the image of my mom comes to my mind. Those countless moments of unrelenting pain and agony which she too had witnessed with me, reminds me of her sacrifice. Only because of her nurture and care, I can rise, walk, talk, and do what I am able to do today. All my physical capabilities and mental faculties, I find them deeply related to my upbringing in her care. She could not control the events, but she did what she could. She stood solidly behind me when I was vulnerable, weak, diseased, or depressed. She has put all her might in helping me grow, recover, learn, and explore the world. She has always guided me in navigating the complex world, teaching us whatever she has learned.

I dedicate this book to none but her.

Contents

FOREWORD

It's a pleasure to write something about *If I can, You too can Survive*, a sort of autobiographical sketch of a Electronics & Communication engineer who claims himself not being a "regular writer" and the purpose of narrating his "story" is to encourage others to overcome the difficulties of their lives as has been done by him. Autobiography is a genre of literature whose origin dates back to at least two millenniums. As put by Helga Schwalm, it is "notoriously difficult to define" and is almost synonymously equated with "life writing" and stands for all modes and genres of telling one's own life. It is a sort of retrospective narrative that tells the author's own life, or a substantial part of it, seeking to "reconstruct his/her personal development within a given historical, social and cultural framework."

Bijoy Ananda Langthasa begins his sketch with an ambivalent note as is common in any autobiographical narrative regarding the starting point, but subsequently takes the readers most eloquently in the journey of some parts of his life. After narrating briefly about his family background and early part of life he straight way comes to the focal point of his life narrative which he intends to share in order to encourage others to take up the challenges of life. The eloquent and flawless narrative takes the reader to delve into the minutest details of his arduous journey from a remote village of southern Assam to the offshore platform in Arabian Sea and his continuous struggle to overcome his chronic diseases. The details of his treatment in different parts of the country and the names of the prescribed medicines that he shares can make any reader feel for the suffering that he underwent. His occasional encounters with fake "religious leaders" (?) gives a sort of comic relief to the readers, but simultaneously brings forth the prevailing practice in the society to dupe common people in the name of religion. The readers feel relieved to see him cured from his chronic disease after getting in touch with a Homeopathic doctor and see him back to his normal life after enduring an arduous journey of sufferings.

Although Bijoy Ananda Langthasa humbly disassociates himself from the category of "regular writer," but the flawless narrative gives the impression of the opposite to his view about himself. The powerful narrative along with his command over the language keeps the interest of the readers sustained and has the potency to feel affinity with his struggle and in this sense this autobiographical narrative serves its purpose as envisioned by him to germinate a sort of belief in others about their own potentiality. Hope the readers will find this narrative interesting as well as useful.

Dr. Anup Kumar Dey
Head, Department of English
Assam University (a Central University), Diphu Campus
P.O. Diphu, Karbi Anglong, Assam

PREFACE

This is not my maiden attempt to pen down something for publishing in form of a book. I have had made many unsuccessful attempts. When I was young, I remember the thought, it was like "I am too young to write a book. I am still learning."

With the sequence events that unfolded in that phase of my life, I have no option but to share my experience of coming out of a period of life, which was just like hell. Sometimes there was no ray of hope, and I was depressed as nothing was working; I was watching my young life fizzling out and seemed I was dying slowly. But I never gave up and my resilience showed result and made me capable enough to share this story with you.

I am not sure where to begin, hence thought of starting in chronological listing of events that happened in that phase of my life. Besides, as I am not a regular writer, not sure of putting an 'eye-catching' tittle to this book, but the whole purpose of narrating my story is to encourage many individuals who all are suffering from one or other diseases as I suffered for a long period in my life. I feel, if a common person like me can overcome those challenging times, then why not others. Hence, I thought of putting a title with which, many, who are suffering from bad phase of life can relate. Someone, who is looking for a list of to-dos or any remedial processes may be disappointed as I personally feel that certain process which is beneficial for an individual may not be so for another. Hence, instead of putting out a 'To-do list,' I have tried to put out my journey from despair to recovery and I believe, with some readjustments anyone can chart their own path of recovery.

Readers may be eager to know my basic details. My birth was to tribal parents in a remote village in Assam. I finished my schooling there in the same village by the year 1995. Thereafter, I studied for two years at Cotton College, Guwahati before joining NIT, Jalandhar (then REC Jalandhar) for Engineering degree. As a tribal student, I got preference in joining the Engineering program and in joining an oil PSU (a Govt. of India Enterprise), which would have been difficult for me otherwise. I have visited many field locations of the PSU, worked at various offices, and presently working at offshore oil processing unit, which is considered as one of the most difficult postings. I also have experience of a year of working in private manufacturing industries. As a pastime, I collaborate closely with the school level educators for facilitating quality education to all.

I have lived a very normal life; marriage, child, all those have happened to me in their own time. Oh, yes, I am a Male and straight (Many times I get proposals from other males, and many ask me my gender). My pastime habits are very wide ranging from software to agriculture. I am a good student in every field of learning. Please do not remind me of the proverb naming 'Jack.' Throughout my life, I have associated myself with many social services works and NGOs and I hope of keeping myself engaged with such activities in future too. I frequently tell my friends in lighter vein, "See, I have got a job which pays me reasonably good, I am happy with my work, I have got a family and relatives, my health is good, and I have also done Insurance to take care of my family when I am not around. Hence, I do not see a single reason I should worry."

I had finished writing the main contents of the book around the year 2017. But publication of this book was delayed as I was looking for ways to publish this book. I have not changed context and content of the main text completed back in the year 2017. Otherwise, I have apprehensions that original emotion and necessity to pen down this book would be lost.

Acknowledgements

My acknowledgement goes deeply to my mom. She had expressed in many ways of her desire to see us embodying the qualities of true human being. I am not sure, where I stand in her expectations, but I am sure, sharing the stories of my struggles with others who may find it as helpful, will be a step in that direction.

My life partner, Sunanda has immense contribution to this work. She used to read and suggest corrections in my writing, as being English literature teacher, she has an upper hand.

My friend Shri Ripunjay Sharma motivated many a times to complete my book and to let it see light of the day.

My friends, coworkers have who always motivated me with their kind words and praises, which were sometimes more than what I deserved. I acknowledge the encouragement of Shri Dheeraj Rawat, Shri AK Satyam, Shri Debesh Ghosh, Shri Sbhubham Sharma, Shri Anupam Bhargawa, Ali Asgar Shouque, Shri Sachin Chauhan, Dr. Himamoni Deka, Dr. Ranjit Timung, Mr. Xavier Kerketa, and many others whose name am not mentioning as I must stop somewhere.

Prof Anup Kumar Dey has been kind enough to write few words for my work. I am highly encouraged and emboldened by his words. I acknowledge his time and effort and more importantly his kindness to go through my work in his busy schedule.

PROLOGUE

I know I have gone through a rebirth. I have not studied Sanskrit but have heard someone explaining why a person is called 'Dwiz' in Sanskrit. As per him, everyone must take two births in life as a human being: first his physical birth and another his realization about his own self. Second birth, i.e., realization of own self is I feel is a continuous process, through which one must go through eventually and there cannot be any end to it; it is just like evolutionary process of the universe. Right now, I am feeling as being treading through the path of second birth.

I will mark the beginning of this story somewhere behind four years, i.e. towards the end of 2011 (now 2015, when I have started writing this piece), the year my place of work was relocated from Sibsagar (in Assam) to MHN Platform at Mumbai offshore (in the waters of Arabian Sea, 90 Nautical miles from Mumbai shores). Almost half a year prior to that my sufferings began to trouble me. I had good acquaintances with abdominal troubles and pains since my birth. Mom used told me that I had cried inconsolably for days after I was born. Clueless about reason of crying, she took me to a homeopathic 'doctor' (and it was the most easily available treatment then in my village) and the 'doctor,' after seeing my condition, declared that I was having stomach pain. My screaming stopped once he administered one dose of his medicines.

Though I might have recovered then; my sufferings persisted throughout. When I was around eight, I had major trouble with Jaundice and Malarial infection. I could survive only because of Mom and my maternal uncle. They took utmost care of mine. I was hospitalised for more than a month at that time and post hospitalization, it took a year to for me to recover. I remember, I was sent to my maternal uncle's place for half a year, and I was put through strict diet regime of bland diet (mostly boiled preparation) of vegetables only, no meat, no fish, no egg, without oil or any spice except turmeric and salt. My mom feared that as she was the only surviving parent to take care of her four children, she might not be able to monitor my meals while she was away on her teaching job. I do not know, at that young age, how I had managed to survive on that simple diet. I can only imagine that I might had been told that that was the only way to survive and to get cured of my illness.

Because of the year long experience, I developed a capability of gorging, anything which is recommended as good for me, regardless of its taste. For that year long, I rarely went out as there was a few whom I knew in that new place, and my activity was limited within the perimeter of the house. I was not a good student, but as I had no one to play with, I concentrated on my textbooks for next session as suggested by Mom and I also put some effort to read few books and comics provided by my uncle. This, I belief, helped me to develop a habit of reading books while I become older.

My uncle and mom are deeply religious persons and strict vegetarians. My young impressible mind caught up with the idea. I followed their path and had become vegetarian since my childhood and followed all the religious rituals they did; but discarded them in the later stage of my life when I got convinced otherwise. But old habits die hard, till date, I still have preference for vegetarian foods.

Although I recovered from the illness, my health remained frail. I was the weakest among my siblings and friends. I kept of struggling with my health, some or the other disease or infection kept on hunting me, cold and sneezing was one regular occurrence for me. My treatment continued; my educational burden also increased. In my school days, one good thing happened that somewhere I read about the benefits of doing Yoga. But in my remote village, there was no one doing Yoga and there was no one to teach me Yoga. Hence, I bought a book from a weekly market in our village and started doing 'Yoga;' doing whatever I could learn from that book. I did not notice whether Yoga was doing good to me or not, but in the book the author had highly praised the benefits of doing Yoga, which was enough for me to keep on doing it religiously. As I recollect, one of my friends commented, "You are looking very healthy in that pic." He was looking to my photo taken just after completing my 10th board exam. Thus, I can fairly conclude that I was gaining something from my 'book' taught knowledge of Yoga.

But after my 10th board exam I went away from home for 10+2 and then engineering, my troubles with health kept on reappearing. In those six to seven years of my important life, I was hospitalized or put on bed rest at least once in every year for digestive system related ailments. My friend become very much familiar with my hospital routines. They often teased me, "When are you going to hospital again?" Some would say, "Yaar, start taking non-veg, you would be cured of everything." After my 10+2, I got a chance to study engineering at NIIT Jalandhar (then REC Jalandhar) in Punjab. I took up the challenge despite my frail health. I might have told to myself, "This is the only way out. Go and win for yourself." I enjoyed my stay there, but my hospital routines remained same. But with help of my friends and well-wishers I could complete my four years degree course in time.

I
Real Trouble

I landed on a job with a reputed PSU in Assam, I was 25 years old at that point of time. Initially my place of posting was Nazira and later I went to Sibsagar. I enjoyed my initial years of posting at those places. The weather was good, except few hot & humid months of Jun & July, when there is a dry spell. It starts raining there from April and continues till October. The rains kept the temperature moderate and hence during the monsoon life becomes very cozy if you are sitting in your office sipping cup of tea of your favourite local flavour. Or the effect is double in the rainy evenings if you sit around with your friends with glasses of local or imported liquor and plates of local river fish or local poultry. The winter is also not too harsh. The whole season of winter starting from November to end of February is considered as the season of picnic. People will go around with friends and family on the banks of rivers like Dikhow, Dishang and Brahmaputra to enjoy the pleasant weather.

The cuisine and people were remarkably familiar to me. As days progressed, I gathered more friends apart from my office circle. With my office colleagues, I used to go for playing golf at Lighiripukhuri golf course, which was owned by our organization. Evenings were for parties or some invitation. As a young bachelor guy, I was invited and accepted everywhere. Friends, Girlfriends, picnics, trips, parties, music and what not, everything was happening to me in those years.

Now, when I try to recollect, yoga must have taken backseat in those years. Golf and other outdoor activities had replaced Yoga. At that time everything was going smooth for me. Work, move and celebrate, this was the norm, I was seeing same happening with everyone. I thought that I too had joined the normal league.

It took me some years to understand that I do not belong to that league. Initially it was minor stomach upset or weakness or fever. Visit a random doctor, get some pills and you are back in action again. Later, I required consultation of some specialists to regain the health. Finally, even the specialists' prescription ceased to work. After eight years of service in Assam, I ended up with acute stomach pain and swollen left wrist in tremendous pain. Doctors' prescription, diet control or exercise, nothing seemed to be helping me getting relief from those sufferings.

Vitamins & antacids had become part of my life. The diets and medicines which had worked on earlier bouts of illness seemed ceasing to work. Even hospitalization and gastroenterologist suggestion did not work. My symptoms had intensified, and my stomach pain had become almost unbearable. In addition to that pain on my left wrist was there. My stomach pain barred me from taking any effective medicine to reduce the wrist pain and the pain on the wrist was increasing day by day. I had taken suggestions from one of my friends who is an orthopaedic, he suggested, after a battery of tests, to take some calcium tablets. There were no conclusive findings to suggest any specific disease. I had understood that I must go to some 'super' specialists.

At that point of time, my left wrist pain and the stomach pain had become my normal companion. If I could bear the wrist pain to some extent, the stomach pain in some days would become unbearable. In addition to that I could not eat properly, most of the food items would increase the stomach pain. I was taking the chance that if I continue taking medicines along with dietary control, at least my stomach pain would subside. Luckily, my younger sister, her pet name is 'Lucky', who was married, somehow managed to come to stay with me for a month along with her two-year-old toddler.

Due to the pain in the left wrist, my left fingers had become immovable. The wrist itself had become extremely sensitive and if I had happened to touch anything with it accidentally, the pain would become unbearable. Little movement with the fingers will give great pain at the wrist. In those days, I had become like a single-handed person, with left wrist bandaged to relieve the pain. I struggled with right hand to do all kinds of routine work; like driving, lifting any item and all other tasks. My visits to the doctor continued; consulted many specialists available there. They recommend multiple tests and medications. My problem was that I had two problems, one was stomach pain and other was the wrist pain. Doctors diagnosed stomach pain as normal acidity as multiple tests like (Endoscopy, Ultrasound, HP parasite) etc. did not yielded any result. I was administered routine antacid drug like Ranitidine, Pantoprazole DSR etc. Still, the pain was persisting combined with loss of appetite and frequent loose motion. A battery of tests was done for the wrist pain also, but the results were inconclusive; the RA (Rheumatoid Arthritis) test result was negative, showed uric acid levels marginally higher. The physician recommended some medicine for controlling uric acid and suggested some diet modification. I was already in vegetarian diet; hence, I stopped taking even milk and pulses.

Consultations were taken from an orthopaedic also; he suggested some medicines but some of those contributed to the increase in stomach pain. I was really like "caught between deep sea and devil." Wrist pain was becoming unbearable; if I would have taken medication for it, the stomach pain would increase two folds. In addition to it, the mental anxiety was increasing with each passing day. I lost kilos of weight and health become very frail. One evening, when I was walking past an acquaintance, he commented after enquiring about my health, "Dear, you are smelling like a box of medicines! Do take care of your health."

I knew my health condition was not good, but when I heard it from someone else it added to the mental load. I was becoming like psychic and was getting overly sensitive to the comments of people around me. Now, I strongly feel we all should be careful about commenting on other's medical conditions. Before saying something to someone who is evidently suffering from some issue, we should ensure that our comment or advise is going to help him. Otherwise, it is better we keep out mouth shut. But you know, at that point of time, I was the sufferer, hence had no option but listen to whatever other says.

I started exploring all the options to the get rid of my illness. One of my friends suggested to visit one of local bone 'expert' who would cure problems using herbs and 'special' technique. I was not a believer in those things but thought of trying it as I was running out of options and other reason for visiting the 'expert' was that he (my friend) had also said that his daughter's problem with one of her legs were cured by that 'expert.' I was told that my friend had consulted all the specialists across India, and nobody could cure her leg but the 'expert'. Thus, I was introduced to the 'expert.'

The behaviour of that 'herbal doctor' (local people call 'kabiraj') did not gave me good impression. He seemed very cunning from his words. He exhibited confidence as if curing my wrist pain was just a simple thing for him. He even said, "One day one guy came rushing to me with his severed fingers; you can see how much people believe in me. But you know, I have chosen to live modest in this small cottage with my family." That fellow lived with wife and son in the outskirts of small town called Sibsagar in Assam.

Self-boasting persons, whether they are boasting their wealth or modesty, are great put-offs for me. As a principle, I try to keep a distance from those, who boasts of himself or his actions. But at that moment my only target was to get rid of that pain. So, I proceeded with his treatment. The 'kabiraj' wrapped my wrist with some clothes, putting some herbs inside and told me keep it that way for few days until my next visit to his place. He took few hundred rupees as fees and asked me to offer prayer at any temple or elsewhere. When he said that offering prayer was most important part of the treatment, my belief further dwindled in effectiveness of his treatment. But still, due to insistence of my friend, I completed the 'treatment' process with few more timely visits with his fees increased from hundreds to a thousand as the number of visits had increased. His final healing process culminated with piercing skin of my left wrist with dried jaws of some fish (probably, catfish) to dispel bad blood. But there was no bad blood (should had been black as he said earlier) oozing out!

That 'treatment' I think, gave me relief for almost one or two hours after its completion. The pain returned and I knew that that was a futile exercise. These incidents, now, when I look in flashback, seems very funny and I find myself as very naïve person at that moment of time. But it also gave me in-person understanding of the desperation of people in general, who often end-up exploited by sorcerers, magical healers or some other 'dhongi baba'(impersonator). There are few more incidents like this one that had happened to me which I will narrate as 'funny' anecdotes.

While writing about these incidents, I remembered one quote of one of my classmates in undergraduate Engineering program at NIT-Jalandhar. He said, "Whatever be the book, reading it doesn't go in waste, we may not like it, but helps us in some stage of life..." About the role of experiences in our lives, to put in his words, "Whatever be the incident, we may like it or hate it, leaves some lesson for us."

In those days, my health was concern for many of our extended family members. Most of the calls would be about my health. In addition to that as I had crossed the age of 30 years, everyone started asking about my marriage plans. When I was asked about health, I could answer all the treatments, I was following up with, but when I was asked about marriage, I used to sweat answering them. I knew that my health was at lowest level and on top of that as a commoner (unlike celebrities freezing eggs, siemens) I had almost crossed higher limit of timely marriage. I used to think, "If my marriage happens few years later, I will be counted among the 'late-marriage' persons". Once the thought of marriage would come, my mind would go into a whirlpool of worries. It started with, "When I will get married?", then "if I want to get married, first I need to find a nice girl", then, "If my health is not okay, how can I find a nice girl?", then, "To find a nice girl, I had to be healthy first", then, "No medicine is working on me, how can I get healthy?", then, "When I will get healthy? When will I get married?" and the cycle continued endlessly. My mind had become restless. I could not sleep in those nights. Nightmares would come in the middle of night, and I would wake up from sleep and would find whole body perspiring profusely. Even now, when I am remembering that phase of my life, I feel the flood of feelings coming back to my mind and my typing speed is no match to rush of emotions even in flashbacks.

It would be difficult for a normal human being to relate to the situation and the emotion surrounding it, if he himself has never experienced such kind of situation where you do not see a ray of hope coming from anywhere. You are trying hard to get out of it, but the situation deteriorates with passing of time and most importantly no one have any solution to it. Such condition is the most depressing, demoralizing and mentally devastating. The feeling I had at that point of time was of a terminally ill persons where everyone had accepted, "Only few more days are left."

I have a friend who is a psychiatric doctor. She was staying at same town in those days. When I discussed some of my issues with her, she advised some psychiatric medicine, most probably Diazepam tablet. I saw, If I had that tablet, I could get some relief from my thoughts and could sleep properly. But again, my cynical mind kicked in. I thought, "I am using a psychiatric drug. What if I become habitual to that drug?" I stopped the drug and told her that I will not have that as there was chance of getting habituated. But she insisted that it was better to have the drug instead of suffering. But I was more interested in curing myself organically without any psychiatric medication. I enquired with her, whether some psychiatric counselling would help. Though she wanted to help, she told me that counselling will not have effect on the person who was her friend. So, the psychiatric thing ended there for time being.

I would often visit home in weekends (overnight journey) or would take few days leave to be with my mom at home. We are four siblings; my elder brother had got married and was living separately, my younger sister was married, and my younger brother was away working in a south Indian state in those days. Our mom had raised four of us as a single parent as dad passed away when I was just a six-year-old kid. Our maternal uncles helped us a lot in many ways till we became independent souls.

It was in the summer of 2011, when I told my boss that I needed a long leave to be at home to get myself healed from all those sufferings. I think I had applied leave for a month and returned home accompanied by the persistent sufferings. The change in surrounding and love and comfort of home had given me relief from the constant pain to an extent. I think, it was when I was done with half of my leave period, I got a mail from our company headquarters informing about my transfer to our company WorkCentre at Mumbai offshore. The letter described that the duty pattern would be on-off (14 days working at sea and next 14 days I am free to do anything with fully paid return air tickets to a place my choice within India). Though I had applied for that transfer earlier, my deteriorating health condition raised doubts about my readiness to cope with harsh working condition at sea. I got a mixed bag of advice from my friends and well-wishers.

I decided to go ahead with transfer order. Few considerations helped me make up my mind. First, I assumed if I were in Mumbai, the access to quality medical care would be easier. (Our organization provides free medical treatment and have agreement with lot of major hospitals in cities to provide cashless treatment to its employees). Second reason was that I would have chance to visit home very frequently without taking any leave. Moreover, I needed a change from my that working environment. I still remember, I had called up one of my old acquaintances, who was already working at offshore location our organization, to enquire about working conditions out there. When he learned about my health condition, he warned, "Bijoy, get rid or all of your diseases before you step in here!"

His advice was short and precise. Our offshore location was in the Arabian sea at west coast of India. The location I was supposed to join was ninety nautical miles (almost 160 km) from the shores of Mumbai in India. The environment itself is harsh and on top of that the workload is tremendous. Most of the work there are physically demanding, and one must work in 12 hours shift pattern. I could understand a storm was gathering in the horizon. And onus was fully on me to take the challenge or run for covers.

Finally, even though single handed (with left hand under wrist guard wrap for protection of wrist), I completed all the formalities at Nazira & Sibsagar offices, packed everything there at Nazira quarters and returned home to dump all my belongings. All my friends helped me bigtime in packing and loading the items. Mr. Pabitra Baro, Mr. Akash Gogoi, Mr. Himangshu Gogoi, Mr. Ranjit Borthakur and few others spent almost one day and night to pack all my belongings and put them in the truck in a safe way. With only one hand available, I could hardly pack or lift anything properly, but they took care of everything on my behalf. I am still indebted to them for that help. I had good bonding with those guys while working at office and they arranged separate farewell function for me apart from the official farewell ceremony. My heart cried for them while moving out of that place. They are still very much in my touch, and we discuss lot of issues related to family or office.

II

Challenge begins

I landed in Mumbai on 11th June 2011. Prior to that I might have gone to that city twice or thrice for several reasons but have not stayed there for long. Hence, the city was almost unfamiliar for me. I had the company of another colleague who too was joining at Mumbai office. To our comfort, my elder brother who was already working at Mumbai was waiting for us at Airport. He took us to all necessary places to complete the formalities and it was smooth process. My mind was preoccupied with my health concern and my senior colleague's advice to get well before stepping into sea was getting repeated in every alternate thought in my mind.

Very next day, I visited our company health consultant, he referred me to a doctor (gastroenterologist) in the famous "Lilavati Hospital" (at Bandra reclamation, Mumbai). The gastroenterologist checked all my reports, recommended some more tests including ultrasound scan of whole abdomen and asked me to consult another orthopaedic doctor at same hospital for my wrist pain. Those few days would later prove to be very crucial for my health and life. Hence, I am trying to describe them as it happened.

I made a visit to the orthopaedic also. He recommended some more tests and MRI of my left wrist. I did all of them, collected the reports and visited the gastroenterologist again. He found nothing abnormal except symptoms of acidity and weight loss. Hence, he recommended an antacid and a multivitamin tablet. Next visit was to the orthopaedic doctor, he checked all my reports along with the MRI scan, he doubted bone cox (Tuberculosis) and started five sets of antibiotics to be taken on daily basis. He also suggested for biopsy of wrist tissues and referred me to one of the best hospitals in Mumbai, Hinduja Hospital, Dadar. He specifically asked for the procedure to be done at Hinduja Hospital only. He advised that the antibiotics were to be taken only after the biopsy procedure. Here, I am refraining from mentioning name of any of the doctors to avoid any kind of controversy. I went to Hinduja Hospital at Dadar, Mumbai, took appointment, which was slotted for two or three days later. I revisited Hinduja hospital as per my allotted slot for the biopsy appointment and after the procedure, I was informed that it will take 21 days to get the final verdict. The doctors in Hinduja were very much unwilling to do biopsy as they had the concern that the procedure will cause permanent damage to my wrist. After speaking with my consulting orthopaedic, they finally conducted the procedure.

As we had come to Mumbai on transfer me and my colleague were allotted hotel room at Andheri (West), near Lallubhai park. Me and my friend were quite amused to find the couples, in the evening hours, sitting in embracing, lip-locked positions in various benches inside the park while they were visible from all the sides. We discussed among ourselves and concluded, "This is Mumbai and here nobody cares what other one is doing!"

Not only the couples in the garden, we saw people lying on the walkways with visibly diseased bodies, but people walked them past exhibiting total ignorance. We realized that unlike in villages or small towns, here in megacities, people were so busy with their work and life that they do not have any time to spare for others. This the reason why the accident victims, in cities, die unattended in the middle of thousands of onlookers. Even if my health was not in decent shape, I ventured along with my colleague to roam around place near the hotel to familiarize with the area. After few days of stay, my colleague left for "Sea Survival" training at Goa (mandatory requirement for working in marine environment).

The orthopaedic doctor had suggested to take the antibiotics after the tissue sample was taken for biopsy. My real trouble began once I started taking those medicines. I was swallowing five antibiotics on daily basis as recommended by him. My stomach, was already in pain, revolted violently as aftereffect of those antibiotics. At the hotel, I could not sleep for two or three nights. The feeling was like something burning inside me and as if there were cut wounds inside my tummy.

I believed that I had extraordinarily strong will power, but at that moment, I felt as if I had no options left but to die. I had to cancel my Goa training program for which I had done all bookings and arrangements. Informed my sectional In-charge about my condition and visited our company chief medical officer at Mumbai whom I had known from the days at Assam. I insisted for hospitalization as I knew that my condition was worsening with each passing day. He spoke to the treating gastroenterologist and requested him for my admission to the hospital.

I am not a physically well-built person, but as I had already mentioned, I kept myself maintained by doing yoga and following good dietary habits. Till to the point of time I was a vegetarian and used to take curd, milk and all those healthy stuffs in abundance. Hence, my fitness level, even in those conditions, was not less than average and I never allowed my physical or mental stress to be visible on my face. When I went to the doctor for admission, he was very reluctant to admit me in the hospital and only after my repeated requests he recommended my admission. I had gone there all alone and hence the hospital stuffs would assume me to be the attendant of a patient and would ask, "Where is the patient?"

Finally, I was admitted in the famous Leelavati Hospitals, Mumbai with the expectations of getting cured of my troubles. Leelavati hospital is till date famous for its celebrity patients. My expectation was quite high. But the doctors did a little. He did routine check-ups and recommended some more tests. Results were same as previous. He recommended to increase the dosage of antacid and multivitamins. The orthopaedic came and advised to continue with his prescription. But my pain did not subside. When I complained of weakness along with pain, a dietician visited and recommended a protein powder, which had to be taken along with milk. After few days of taking that protein power, my appetite was gone, my tummy swelled, and indigestion kicked in. In that condition, I stayed for almost ten days and finally doctor came and told me to get discharged. As my condition had not improved, I asked him, "Will I be able to regain my health?"

He said, "Do not worry! You will be able to run in marathons." After hearing his answer, I had not had much to say and hence, I returned to my company Guest house. My condition was same as when I got hospitalized. Post discharge, I was swallowing a greater number of antacid capsules along with the five dosages of antibiotic.

Next day, I met my sectional In-charge and told him that I am ready to go to offshore. I requested him to arrange my journey to MHN platform (my workplace), in the middle of Arabian sea, in the next available helicopter sortie. Hence, day after morning, I found myself travelling, for the first time in a helicopter, to my designated platform. My body was diseased, burning from inside, but I made up my mind and was ready to explore what comes next. This attitude has not deserted me till now and I believe it has brought me where I am today.

The first experience of anything is very pristine. The thrill of helicopter travel made me forget everything else for that time being. On top of that I was seeing that vast expense of water body from above for the first time. I repeatedly edged over my seat to look down below as much as possible. Blue water below, blue sky above and in the middle, we were cruising effortlessly! Everything looked so beautiful. At some point of time, the pilot, seeing my never-ending enthusiasm, asked me to calm down and sit relaxed. When we landed at platform, the pilots were surprised to know me as an employee of the organization. They confessed to the radio officer,

"We were thinking that he was kid of some big boss in the organization, and we were also thinking of the way-out to bring our wards for such an experience!"

Here its pertinent to disclose that the offshore oil rigs and platforms are high security zones and no person, except employee or person permitted by Govt. of India, can visit those locations.

The offshore rigs are known to the most; they drill thousands of meters below the bottom of the sea (seabed) to tap the hydrocarbon storage at those depths. On the other hand, the offshore platforms extract the hydrocarbon resources tapped by rigs. Pipelines are laid from the drilled oil well locations to offshore platforms to carry the mix of water, gas, and oil, which is called as crude oil. There in that platform, the gas, water, and oil, are separated by various processes and then the gas and oil are pumped through pipelines to another installation on land. The water is further processed, decontaminated to certain recommended level, and released back to the sea.

Another important process is the water injection into certain depths of formation, in which the sea water is passed through stages of filtration and deoxygenation systems and those treated seawater is pumped into dry oil wells to maintain the formation pressure. Those water injection water are in three stages and maintain extremely high pressure (around 150 $kgcm^{-2}$).

These platforms at offshore, where this type of processing takes place, are also called process platforms. Some platform locations are used only for gathering of crude oil & gas pipelines and no permanent manpower is stationed there. Hence, they are called 'Unmanned' platforms. Routine visits are planned from nearby process platforms to the unmanned platforms for their upkeep and maintenance.

Most of the manpower movement from one location to another is managed through Helicopter sorties. For goods and material supplies logistics ships are engaged. The food supplies are sent from base every week to each of the process platforms. During monsoon season the ships movement gets disturbed; hence organization advises the process platform in-charges to maintain enough quantity of dry food stocks.

Before coming to the platform, I had little idea of the type of work at offshore process platforms. Leave alone the offshore platforms, I had only theoretical idea about the oil and gas business as my work was limited to Information Technology and IT facility management at the Assam offices of our organization. There at platform, my assignment was as an Instrumentation Engineer, about which also I had extremely limited idea. Seeing my experience, before sending me to offshore, when I was completing formalities, one of the senior officers in base office enquired about my experience and asked me, "Do you know what the work of an instrumentation engineer are at offshore?"

"No, sir!" I replied to his astonishment.

He then gave me long stare and asked again, "How will you work then?"

Me with full of confidence, replied to him, "I will learn within a month."

"One month, I will be very happy if you can learn the tricks even in a year." He said to me like throwing a challenge.

I smiled to him and accepted his challenge. In my mind, I knew with my given health conditions, which was going to be though.

After reaching platform, I was just like a fish out of water. Whole platform was jungle of steel and metals. I had no idea about a single piece out of them. There was shortage of manpower in the instrumentation section, hence the employees of the platform were incredibly happy to see me as an addition to the instrumentation team. The expectation from me, for reasons unknown (at that time, which I learned later) to me, were remarkably high. I was received by the section In-charge, he introduced me to all the other sectional In-charges and managers. When he finally led me to instrumentation section, I confided in him that I know nothing about the jobs that would be assigned to me. He said nothing, opened some folders in the computer and indicated towards some .pdf files, he said, "Do not worry many persons like you have come here. If you wish to learn and work, then you can obviously do wonders."

I figured out that those .pdf files will be handy in understanding basic instruments and the systems. By his encouragement, I started with those .pdf files and tried to gain as much possible from other team members. But even after putting lot of efforts, true to the prophesy of the senior officer at base, it took me almost a year to gain some understanding of the complete instrumentation systems at offshore platform.

After few years at that platform, one of my seniors told me that someone in our organization in Assam, where I worked earlier, reported to them me as very tech savvy and efficient person with good dressing sense. When he revealed that to me, I felt very ashamed as could not match their expectations in my initial days at the platform. But the platform people were very much considerate and ignored my early mistakes as my learning efforts.

To my own estimates, the learning time should not have gone beyond six months, but my health was going to play key role in my learning process. I went there with a bag full of medicines, antacids, multivitamins, antibiotic, and some other SOS medicines. I met the catering manager there and asked him to prepare bland diet for me. He promised at least boiled lentils and boiled vegetables. I had lost all the appetite because of the heavy dosages of medicines. I could not find any taste in the food. The antibiotics were giving me real trouble, pain in stomach increased with every dose. I could not stop having them also as the doctor had told me that if I had missed any of the doses, I would have to start from beginning. Because of pain, I had spent many sleepless nights. Even if I had slept, I would wake up from nightmares, my whole body would get wet with sweat. The problem of nightfall had become very frequent in those days. In the morning, my body would be drained of energy, would feel sleepy throughout the day, little bit of exertion would make me tired.

In this condition, I returned to Mumbai after completing 17 or 18 days of offshore duty. Rushed to the Hinduja Hospital for the final report. Report was conclusively negative about any strain of Tuberculosis bacteria. The orthopaedic sheepishly asked me to stop the antibiotics and asked me to do Anti-CCP antibody test (It is as confirmatory test for Rheumatoid Arthritis). The Anti-CCP test results showed elevated level of antibody and hence he started some steroid and some other drugs for treatment of RA (Rheumatoid Arthritis).

I was both happy and angry at my situation. I was happy and felt relieved that I am not suffering from tuberculosis, but the diagnosis procedure of the doctor made me feel very helpless. I was thinking why that fellow had not chosen to do Anti-CCP test earlier along with all the other tests. It was just a blood test. His simple carelessness led me to pay such a heavy price with my health. But the carelessness did not end there only, we would come to understand that in later stages. I felt like being cheated by the doctor, but nothing was in my hand, and I had many other problems to attend too. Hence, I returned home with the medicines for RA and my stomach pain.

The medicines for RA showed effect, my wrist pain subsided in a few days. But I was aware that the steroidal drugs I was having was not safe, it had lot many side effects. I got relief from the pain in the wrist but not from the stomach. On my return journey to Mumbai for attending offshore duty, I consulted both doctors. The orthopaedic altered some of the doses, while the gastroenterologist had nothing much to do. After the visit, I went to offshore and completed my duty. This way, I completed two or three shifts, each shift numbering 14 days of duty at offshore and 14 days at home including the travel period. The RA medicine had started showing symptoms on my body.

Weakness, pain, and anxiety was ever present. I too did not give up the fight, I continued attending duty at offshore. But the quality of work, I could deliver, was extremely poor. I could not walk much distance from office. Most of the time, I just remained mute observer while my other colleagues worked. I could not concentrate on anything. I would feel sleepy in the middle of any serious discussions. As a newcomer, not much of work was expected from me but I could not work to the satisfaction of myself. My In-charge was starting to get upset with my performance. Many times, he would ask me to accompany him for some work, but I would simply show some excuse to hide m physical weakness. They all knew I have some illness, but nobody could understand the seriousness seeing my courageous face.

In the month of Nov'2011, my flight from Guwahati to Mumbai was on the next day. I normally come one day in advance by evening train to Guwahati from my village. I packed everything, had lunch, got the bag ready, dressed up and said bye to everyone. I lifted bag, I do not remember what happened, I started crying and said to mom who was standing nearby, "I won't be able to go today." Tears rolled down my cheek. I was feeling like being cornered, left with no escape route. Thoughts come to my mind at that moment, "Even super-specialist doctor from Mumbai cannot treat my stomach pain and medicine for wrist pain is killing me. What is left for me? Death! It is better to die at home." I was tired of acting to others that everything is all right with me.

"If you are feeling like not going, then don't go, take rest for more days," my mom said calmly.

I looked out for my platform's landline number and called up my In-charge and told him in emotionally loaded voice that my health was not allowing me to go to the platform. He too assured me and told me to take rest until I was fit enough to return to workplace. Me and mom sat silently in her bedroom for quite few moments. She knew that I had some trouble, but she was not much concerned as I was taking treatment from 'good' doctors in Mumbai. Me too never gave full details of whatever happening with me just not to burden her with worries. She was more concerned with my marriage; she believed my marriage would have solved lot many problems of mine. She was surprised but kept cool and calm demeanour. Later in the evening, I called up one of my sister's friend Dr. Himamoni Deka to discuss my possible treatment options. I remembered she had once mentioned about a gastroenterologist in Delhi. She gave me the doctor's personal number. I called up the doctor the other day and explained my problem in short to him. He asked told me to visit him and more importantly he said that my both problems (wrist & stomach pain) might be interrelated. His words gave me some ray of hope and I was hearing for the first time that cause of both the problems could be one.

I knew that the reimbursement of medical expenses from my company for treatment done at Delhi would be difficult as Mumbai city had all the facilities at par with Delhi. But when death seems to be lurking around the corner, one does not think much about money or other worldly matters. In a few days, I fixed the appointment with the doctor, booked ticket for me and our youngest maternal uncle (we call him 'mama' and he is the person who took utmost care of us in all the difficult times) and took off to Delhi.

The doctor, Dr. Anil Arora, an alumnus of AIIMS and many reputed institutes, was then Chairman of Sir Gangaram Hospital's Gastroenterology and Hepatology Department and he has many awards to his fame. He had maintained some private practice along with his official assignments. He swiftly finished my diagnosis, blood test, ultrasound, endoscopy and more importantly colonoscopy. Every specialist, I visited earlier, recommended endoscopy, but none had done colonoscopy. On top of that Dr. Arora also done some 'double-balloon-endoscopy,' which is deep penetrating imaging of small intestine. It occurred to my mind at that point of time, "AIIMS tag does matter!"

The verdict was out within a few days, which made me both happy and worried. Dr. Arora said that I was possibly suffering from Crohn's disease and Rheumatoid arthritis, and both are autoimmune diseases. (For unversed, Autoimmune disease is not caused by any external microorganism or any substance but own body's immunity starts attacking healthy body cells causing another type of disease. In other words, it is abnormal behaviour of body's immunity, triggered by reasons unknown.) He showed that there are multiple ulcers in my colon and minor erosions in my small intestines. The diagnosis made me happy because for the first time someone had new name for my suffering. But as I was told that those were autoimmune diseases and I would have to take medicines for lifetime, that caused lot of stress in my mind.

He recommended Tab. Pentasa 500mg (6 tab. daily), Tab. Normaxin 5 mg (2 tab. daily), Folvite (1 tab daily), another tablet for Calcium & D3. When I asked about next check-up date, he said that there was no need to come to Delhi and he gave me contact no. of one of his juniors at Guwahati. Quite satisfied I returned home with stock of medicines for two to three months. The Pentasa Tab. was somewhat costly, one strip was costing around INR 250.00 to 300.00 in those days, and I needed six strips in every 10 days. I had an assumption that the typical medicine would not be available in Assam except Guwahati. Hence, I stoked up the medicine for few months with thought in my mind, "I need to live at least another five years as few important goals of my life are yet to be completed."

After consultation with that Delhi doctor, I stopped that RA medicine prescribed by the Mumbai doctor as the pain in the wrist had reduced significantly and I continued with the new set of medications. My stomach problem too started showing some improvement, but the general weakness and lack of appetite remained the same. My weight dropped to 57 kgs (my weight peaked to 72 kgs in the year 2009). Wherever I was going, I was carrying bag full of medicines. When I told others about me not feeling hungry all the time, some of them would joke, "After taking so many medicines, how will you feel hungry!"

Few others would say, "Your medicines weigh more than you, how do you manage to lift them!"

My frail health, series of hospitalization, repeated leaves, and that also in new unaccustomed working environment, I felt like, I was becoming a matter of ridicule for most of them. Yet, something inside me kept on asking to tread ahead. Many times, I wanted to commit suicide by jumping in the sea water or prayed to God for some sort of air crash incident. Whenever the thought of suicide came to my mind, again some part of my mind will say, "Let us wait for few more days. Let us keep that option for the last."

Every day in the morning, I would wake up and would compare the situation with previous day. If I saw slight improvement than I would say to myself, "I have improved by 0.1% today..." That would give me motivation to strive for few more days. This habit continued till I gained reasonably good health.

I started to compromise with the reality of the moment that I would have to live with these medicines
if I wished to remain alive and hence was taking them religiously. I was living with new normal and had accepted that as my destiny. Suddenly, after two or three months, while I was there at the platform, there were red rashes all over my body, especially on the lower part of body. The on-board doctor could not specifically tell what type of skin disorder that was. He gave some anti-allergic medicine and ointment for local application. But the condition deteriorated within two or three days, and I was sent to Mumbai for further treatment. I again went to Lilavati Hospital, this time to visit the dermatologist. The medicines prescribed by him helped me in getting rid of the medicines within a week, but his casual approach proved detrimental for me, and his diagnosis would be proved wrong later. He told me that the rashes on my body were because of the reaction of the Tab Pentasa. I called up the Delhi doctor and explained him the situation. He told me if the dermatologist says so then stop the tablet and asked me to consult his junior in Guwahati.

On reaching Guwahati, I consulted the doctor suggested by the gastroenterologist in Delhi, he gave me some other alternative medicines. Those medicines were not so effective as Tab. Pentasa, my symptoms starter rising their head again. Weakness & lack of appetite was always there, wrist pain was there in moderation, but stomach pain kept on increasing with each day. But something within me kept me leading forward, not allowing me to lose the battle so easily.

I returned to platform as per schedule in the next shift. One night, while I was sleeping, (sound sleep
had become exceedingly rare in those days), I dreamt a very

frightening scene. In my dream, I dreamt myself being lowered into a grave with help of ropes and saw people were looking at my dead body. I woke up very much frightened; found my whole body was wet from profuse sweating and heart was beating fast. I sat up on the bed, climbed down to floor (we in platform has upper and lower bed like 2nd AC train compartments), sipped water from a bottle on the table, went to toilet and returned to bed. Many thoughts came to my mind, but one of them, I still remember, was, "This is not an ordinary dream. The dream is indication that I am at a possible turning point in my life..."

Rest of the night, till I fell asleep, the thought about the dream bothered my mind. I thought that the way things were happening to me can lead me to certain death very soon. I realized that as my health would deteriorate, I would be bedridden soon and once bedridden, I would die a painful death. I asked myself in thought, "Should I allow that to happen?"

"Never," said another corner of my mind.

After whirlpool of different thoughts and worries, I decided in my mind, "I will make this night the real turning point in my life. I will do only those things which are good for my health and will do in best possible way. Let me use full of my remaining energy only to become more energetic and healthier."

The decision led me to make a strategy. The strategy was wholistic. First was treatment. Since, I was already consulting many good doctors, there was not much to do, but I planned that I would keep on knocking all avenues where I can get effective treatment. Second was diet, I resolved that I would consume only healthy and easily digestible foods. Third was the exercise to increase fitness. I was doing yoga regularly, but I did not learn that from any professional teacher. I felt that I needed to consult a yoga guru. That I kept for my next off-duty cycle. Fourth was my mental state. I decided to listen to various motivation talks as well as read various motivational books. With these four-pronged strategy, I felt a new motivation to fight the problem at hand and I became more determined to win the battle.

Now, when I narrate these incidents as flashback, leave alone others, even I find surprised that I had gone through such horrific and compelling situations. It seemed to me, at that time that all the escape doors are getting closed one after another. Those were the toughest testing days where a single mistake of consuming unhealthy item or a little disturbance in sleep caused devastating effect to my health. Moreover, following a tight health regime is not that simple. You need to constantly watch what are you eating. During travelling and while moving to different work locations, the 'safe' food items are not always available. I needed to plan for all three meals of the day. For maintaining Yoga practices, I needed to get up early in the morning and for that I had to sleep early in the night. A little disturbance here and there would upset whole weeks program. Sometimes it happened that I could not stop myself and eat something out of the lure of taste, which should have not been eaten otherwise. I had to suffer consequences of that mistake for many days.

III

Fighting Back

Discontinuing Tab Pentasa caused the old symptoms to reappear in my digestive system. My stomach pain started, indigestion kicked in and loss of appetite became prevalent again. Whatever improvement I had seen with that medication, seemed to be reversing as I stopped taking Tab Pentasa.

It was during Jan-Feb of 2012, I was in the middle of my fourteen days shift at my platform. I started experiencing severe pain in my stomach. None the medicines I was taking at that time was showing any effect on reducing the pain. I impatiently waited for the two weeks to be over and after completion of my shift I boarded next available chopper to Mumbai.

Immediately after getting down from helicopter at Juhu Helibase, Mumbai from offshore, I rushed to the office of chief medical officer of our organization and asked for his suggestion on my condition. After hearing everything from me patiently, "Bijoy, this time I will send you to a very nice doctor." he told me with his kind voice.

I rushed to Kokilaben Dhirubhai Ambani Hospital (KDAH) to meet Dr. Subhash Agal, head of the Gastroenterology and Hepatology section the in KDAH. My old reports were always kept ready at Mumbai for any eventuality. After seeing my reports and previous treatments, he just said, "I don't think the rashes on your body were because of Tab Pentasa."

I became very curious, "Why you are saying that?" I asked him "The dermatologist had asked me to stop that tablet!".

He replied calmly, "Any medicine doesn't take two months to show up reactions, it shows up within 24 hours.".

"Bingo!" my heart missed few beats in joy. "What a common sense this guy has!" I said in my heart.

The dermatologist of Lilavati Hospital appeared as very dumb and ignorant fellow. He (Dr. Subhash Agal) did not do any test, advised me to continue the medicines from the doctor in Delhi and asked to visit him in two months for further assessment. Mentally, I ticked the first point (out of four-pronged strategy) with remark "some progress made."

Second was Diet, by then, I was following strict diet regime. But I kept my window open and searched everywhere for best diet plans. I started following ayurvedic recommendations like, not eating some items in the night like leafy vegetables, high protein items, sour items etc. I avoided milk but was having curd & butter milk in plenty. I was also taking fibrous fruits like sweet lime, apple etc. I kept on gorging and refining food related information each day. Yes, I also started taking sweet water fish and egg by then. Those are the days when I become a non-vegetarian.

For exercise, I had chosen Yoga. I made a mission to find out a Yoga teacher in my neighbourhood in Assam. Those days Swami Ramdev was the most sought-after yoga guru. I thought of going to his ashram and booked a slot in program at Patanjali Yoga Peeth in Haridwar. But I cancelled same later as I was not physically confident enough to be able to sustain the program schedule at such faraway place from home. The thought occurred to me, "If not Babaji (Baba Ramdev), then why not to try one of his disciples."

I took the help of internet to find out Baba Ramdeva school of Yoga teacher nearest to my place. Luckily, I found one at Nagaon, which is just fifty kilometres from my place. I spoke to him over phone and explained my condition. Realizing my urgency, he agreed to teach me directly at his residence.

Thus, there was progress in my strategy in second and third direction. Now, for fourth point, I sat in front of TV. I was watching the channels like Aastha, Sanskar, every day in the morning from 6:00 AM to almost 8:00 AM and in someday up to 10:00 AM.

The routine, I set for myself, was:

1. First get up before 6:00 AM clean face and mouth and then start drinking lukewarm water from my copper jug sitting in front of the TV (I do not brush in the morning as I do brush of my teeth before going to bed in the night).

2. After drinking one and half or two litres of water, slowly sipping from glass, I will go to toilet and will take bath.

3. Start doing Yoga schedule of one and half hour minimum, while listening to various discourses by many Gurus like Baba Ramdev, Swami Balkrishanji, Swadhvi Rithamvara, Shri Sudhanshu ji, Sant Rajinder Singhji, Guruma Anandamurti, Sri Morari Bapuji, Jain guru, Sri Sri Ravishankar etc.

This schedule continued for many years, till birth of my daughter. After her birth, I had to dedicate my morning hours for her care.

One friend of mine, Shri Krishna Kotta, had gifted me few books in those days, two among them is "Celebrating Silence" – by Sri Sri Ravishankar, "Mystic's Musings (Spirituality, Mysticism, Yoga)" - by Sadhguru. I had taken those books from him but was not much inclined to go through them initially. But then my attitude changed, and I was willing to devote some time in those books to see if they can help. I started to read those two books and followed them in letter and spirit. Besides those, I had gone through many other self-help books too, few among them are, "Fish Tales"- By Stephen C. Lundin, Harry Paul, and John Christensen; "A note to Sincere seeker"-By Sri Sri Ravishankar; "The Story of my experiment with Truth"- by MK Gandhi, etc.

As I followed that strict procedures and diet regime as per my four-pronged strategy, my comparative counter started showing positive results. I have already mentioned that I used to compare my health condition each morning with what was on previous day. Someday, I would say to myself, "It is one percent improvement. Good job done! One percent in one day is excellent."

On another day, I would say, "Today there is no improvement!" or "It's negative 0.5 percent."

After few months, I would see improvement in my physical condition in comparison to few months earlier. I was having all those drugs, but somewhere in my mind I was realizing that I could not continue for long with those medicines. I was looking for alternative strategies.

One day, seeing my poor health, one of my senior colleagues recommended me to visit an ayurvedic doctor in Mumbai, who had cured one of his friends, who also had same type of problem as mine. I called up his friend and got the contact information of the ayurvedic doctor. Along with the number, he passed on one essential information. He enquired whether I was doing Yoga, and he stressed that Yoga would play especially significant role in my way to good health. He also recommended me to learn Yoga from "Art of Living"- a foundation by Sri Sri Ravishankar. His advice proven to be immensely helpful later in my life.

I took appointment with the Vaid (Ayurvedic Doctor). He checked my reports, took my wrist on his hand to check my health status and would write prescriptions for me. But the prescription would be retained by his assistance after issuing medicine and they would hand over the slip for next visit. I used to take medicines from them for one to two months dosages. Every visit costed me around INR 2000.00 to INR 3000.00. But they will neither give me the receipt nor the prescription. He would tell me that all the medicines were made by himself. There would be always rush at his centre. I had to wait for two to three hours for my turn to come in every visit. Not issuing prescription or receipt would always create a doubt in my mind, but the recommendation from a person, who got cured of same type of ailment as mine was the strongest reason for me to continue. There in the clinic, I met few other patients who too was getting relief from the doctor. But anyhow all those were in

Mumbai, and in Mumbai, "anything is possible."

I continued his medication, but my situation was neither improving nor deteriorating in my comparison 'meter.' Not going in worse way was incredibly good for me at that moment as I could save myself from consuming the lethal medicine like "Pentasa."

An incident happened at home front. I was relaxing at home after returning from Mumbai. It must be first half of 2012. Out of sudden, my maternal uncle, about whom I have already mentioned, came rushing to our place and packed all of us into a vehicle. He loaded the car with me, mom, and other relatives of us and took us to nearby town named Hojai. On the way he revealed that he is taking us to one of most prominent priests from Varanasi and because of our great fortune only, we would get the chance to have his darshan. He said that the priest could tell past, present and future of any individual. The priest had already seen him (uncle) and have predicted to him that he (uncle) had "Rajyoga," which meant, as per him, that he (uncle) would be soon holding some powerful public position.

Hearing about the priest, I suddenly felt a rising anger in my mind as I have seen many like the cheating people here and there and thought he would not be different. But said nothing to them and accompanied them to the place the priest was staying. First turn was one of my relatives, looking sharply at my relative, he (Priest) said," You have one daughter, right?"

I was thinking, "Who was the bugger that had passed on that info to him?"

"Your wife is expecting, and you will have a son this time." said the priest and touched my relatives' forehead.

He was surprised that whatever that Priest had said about his past and present was true, and the future prediction is so promising. So, he was like he had got everything in the world, and he touched the feet of that priest and handed him a hundred rupees note. I thought, "Now, I got a point to evaluate this priest. After few months we will get to know its Boy or Girl!"

But I was still worried about his source of information about our family.

Next was my mom's turn. He saw my mom and he said something about her health and some other things which made her incredibly happy, and she too handed over hundred rupees to the priest. I too moved forward for my past, present and future prediction. But suddenly a group of people came and insisted the priest that they be seen first as they had some other urgent work. As I had no problem and was starting to enjoy the drama unfolding in front of me. The priest proceeded with their future prediction. I did not hear their discussion but was watching their activity keenly. But what attracted my attention was their bargaining with the priest for the 'fees' after consultation was over. I saw they were giving him twenty rupees or something, but the priest was asking for more. Finally, I saw them settling for Forty Rupees. That worsened my impression about the entire process, and I thought, "See, we village guys are easily getting cheated by happily handing over a hundred rupees note to the priest, without any protest, but this town guys are offering only twenty rupees."

My turn came and I moved forward reluctantly to seek his consultation. Before he said something, my mom pleaded from behind, "Panditji, please see when his marriage will happen."

He looked sternly at my face and announced looking at others, "All of you move outside, now."

I was surprised at his behaviour. He said to his lieutenant, "You too go outside, only Mother and Son will be here."

I was guessing what the matter was. I wondered what such confidential matter he wanted to discuss with us and that is too with that much of secrecy.

As per his wish all others to moved outside. Just three of us, me, mom, and the priest were inside the room. I became curious, "What the hell! Is he going to do any process right now?" I thought.

The priest called my mom nearer and whispered in her ears, "We will have to do puja for your second son."

Mom looked towards me; I said, "Puja, okay, we can do it, no problem."

He looked towards me and said, "This would be a special puja, and it will cost twenty-five thousand rupees."

I was already observing all the activities since beginning, hearing his last sentence, I felt, in my mind, like giving him a tight slap on his fluffy cheeks. But I maintained my composure and said, "Panditiji, we will think about it. Namaste!"

I do not remember how much 'fees' I paid to him, but I immediately moved out of the room along with my mom.

While returning home, mom insisted that we should do the puja regardless of cost. My simple argument to her was, "I earn enough to spend twenty-five thousand rupees for a puja which will ensure my marriage and wellbeing, and I am ready to spend more that, even one lakh rupees, if that is so helpful. But puja can happen with a single petal of flower also, then, what is the point in such costly puja?"

She could not that argument of mine and the chapter closed there.

This episode left me with sympathy for so many people who get cheated by 'priest' like him. For any intelligent and experienced fellow, it is quite easy to gauge the physical condition of person like me who is suffering from incurable ailments for years. The one, who is suffering so much, gets ready to pay anything to anybody who can convince him with his glib talk and some pretensions. This sort of crime happens in our country every day here and there. Yes, my readers will be amused to know that my relative have two kids now, and both are, luckily, girls!

After few weeks, I narrated this incident to one of friends at offshore, he laughed and told me to do 108 times daily recitation of "Mahamrityunjaya Mantra" instead of doing the puja. I said to him, "Wow! Why will I pay rupees twenty-five thousand to someone when I am getting this 'Jnan' (piece of advice) of Varanasi standard free of cost."

Both of us laughed at that. Though, I took that in lighter way at that moment. Later, I thought, "Why not I give it a try?" and I started practising and was practising that until I came across something different. As far as I can understand that practice helped me as something to hold on to while I was going through a hopeless phase.

IV

Re-Hospitalization

I have forgotten the count how many times I was admitted in hospital till to the year 2013. One of that was in second half of year 2012. I was at the same offshore platform, where I had landed first time in offshore, around ninety nautical miles into sea (roughly 160 km), from Mumbai shore. My health deteriorated all sudden, for three days or more, I was not passing motion, could not eat anything, pain increased and had become very weak. The onboard MBBS checked my health and recommended for immediate evacuation to Mumbai for treatment.

I got admitted at KDAH (Kokilaben Dhirubhai Ambani Hospital) to be treated under Dr. Subhash Agal, who had treated me earlier too. He knew the half of story; I truthfully narrated how I had tried my luck with the Ayurvedic doctor and a Homoeopathic doctor in Mumbai.

In the tumultuous events of my life in those days, I had tried Homoeopathic medicines one of the reputed groups in Mumbai. I had high hope on the homoeopathic treatment, as many individuals had told me that Homoeopathy is best for permanent cure to the ailments and there is no side effect. But it did not work for me, and I had to stop after trying for almost three months.

I was there in the hospital for more than a week. My elder brother came and stayed with as an attendant in the hospital. Dr.

Subhash Agal deftly normalised my condition and did all the tests again. The mere presence of someone whom you trust brings huge positive effect. During those days when I went to visit Dr. Agal, when I would see him, literally, host of my problems would disappear immediately. I think, it happens with most of the patients and when they meet their trusted doctors.

After the tests he informed me that not much of the ulcers were left in my guts. He had a doubt that I should not had that much of suffering, because what he had found in diagnosis did not indicate much trouble. Hence, he recommended for an opinion from a psychiatrist. I was like, "OMG, what is this new again. I have become a psychiatric case?"

I said to myself, "I can't have psychological disorder."

I remember, logic, somewhere inside my mind said faintly to me, "Each mad man thinks they are OK."

The psychiatrist, a nice young man, came to my cabin and evaluated me. I was worried and hence bombarded him with all my questions and doubts. He assured that taking psychiatric consultation did not mean that I had become a psychiatric case. As per his assessment, my symptoms were like a case of psycho-somatic disorder. He advised me some drugs and told me to take those regularly as advised. I was quite relieved after his assurances.

After the hospitalization, the packets of ayurvedic 'preparations' disappeared from my bag of medicines and Tab. Pentasa made a comeback with his psychiatric cousins. I was taking those psychiatric medicines with great fear as I thought I might get habituated, even though the doctor had denied of any such possibility.

My elder brother, who was also serving at offshore at that period, as I have already mentioned, was staying with me in the hospital cabin. He was too concerned about state of my health and tried to gather information from all sources for better treatment of my diseases. Seeing me getting hospitalized regularly at least once in every six months, he was fearing for my life. But he was happy to see my "never give up" attitude.

After around ten days in the hospital, I was discharged and was asked to see them in another two months. Together with my brother, we returned home.

My resolve to get better was not shaken till then. On reaching home, I thought of giving a try to the Yoga methods of the "Art of Living" organization. I looked up internet sources, found some numbers and started calling up them. Within a few calls, I got connected to the right person who is not so far away from my place. I requested him for arranging a training program at my location. He too responded enthusiastically and visited our locality along with few other volunteers working for Art of Living organization. My mother arranged lunch for them at my home. They told me to arrange for 30 to 40 participants and a hall for the program. They also told me the course would have some fees, and every participant would have to pay the fees.

The fee was not too high. With help my friends, we gathered around forty persons willing to pay and participate in the course. In rural setup, it is tough to collect fees from persons for a program based on Yoga, as most of them are habituated in getting free 'dollops' from Govt. as well as other NGOs working in those areas. Nevertheless, those friends of mine were influential in that area and hence we could arrange that program in a comparatively short notice period. The program happened within one or two months of our first meeting. I was so happy to see the program happening at my village. I participated with full enthusiasm.

In the second day of program, something happened which troubled me mentally lot even in days later. Even today, I am not able to figure out how should I have responded at that moment. The incident was insignificant, and everyone affected by that may have forgotten that, but I still feel that it would have been better if that incident did not happen altogether. The friend of my senior colleague, who recommended, had extremely high regard for this program. I also had seen Sri Sri Ravishankar in many videos, where he, in his cool and calm demeanour, responds to every question coming his way. In the media too, he was one of the key spiritual personalities getting high publicity in those volatile days of nationwide anti-corruption agitation (Anti-Corruption Agitation in 2012-13). The teacher for our program, who happened to be a lady, was his messenger for us and quite obviously we had high levels of regards and high expectation from her. On the top of all, at that moment that I was the person who needed the program the most.

The program was held during January or February of 2013. It was named as "Art of Living Workshop, Part-I" (now they have renamed it as "Happiness Program"). The first day went off smoothly with great enthusiasm; most of the participants arrived in time but the teacher herself was late to the venue due to some issue. But the people were considerate, given the fact that she arrived only on the previous night to the place and was she was comparatively new to the place. On the second day, some of the participants come a bit late. Initially, she allowed most to join the program but later she asked other volunteers not to allow the participants inside the hall. This deprived some of the interested persons, including my mom, from joining the programs. In rural setup, to join the program, the ladies of the house needed to arrange few of the minimum things before coming for joining the program at 6:00 AM in the morning and which would last for more than two hours. Few of the ladies were coming from the distance of five kilometres or more. Mode of transportation, in rural area is either to walk or use cycle, if you do not have anyone to drop you to the venue. Most of the participants, who were barred, on second day, to enter the workshop hall were the ladies. Some were old, some had toddlers, and some were single women coming from far distance.

When they were stopped at the entry point, I looked at them from my position inside the hall and thought of allowing them into the hall. I was among the organizers and hence responsibility laid with me to manage the situation. I become uncomfortable and was about the ask the teacher to allow them into the hall. Sensing my mental condition, the teacher called out to me, "Bijoy, please focus on the process."

I said to her, "Sister, please allow them inside," pointing to the people outside.

She said that she could not let them in as they were late. I countered that there was hardly 10-15 minutes of delay.

She asked me, "You go to catch the train, and you are late by only 5 minutes, will that do?"

My heart pained hearing her brutal reply.

"Sister, train is made of metals, but we are not made of metals. We are humans!" I said as I believed they should have been allowed to participate.

She did not directly reply to me but also did not allow those participants to join the program. On the later part of the program, she lectured on necessity of timeliness and discipline in our life.

I never meant that there should be no discipline, but my only request was to consider things from human perspective. Those elderly person showing interest and turning up early morning itself was a great achievement for us. Now, it will be great discouragement and sort of injustice to deny them from participation merely because they were late by ten to fifteen minutes. Till date, I am not able to get out of that feeling of guilt.

Later, people indicated to me that she herself was late on first day and no declaration was made by her about possible disqualification for the late arrivals from the second day onwards. I was disheartened; I said to myself, "I should have stressed more for inclusion of those elderly participants, who were late by just 10-15 minutes."

I found myself lacking, as one of the organizers, for not being able to include them in the remaining part of the program. One of the participants, who were barred, was my mom. She was upset that, given the age of her (she was 65 years by then), she was not shown any leniency, while she herself had cooked lunch for the teacher and other volunteers when they came for the first time to our place.

I, considered many times in my mind, thought of complaining about the unfortunate event to management of "Art of Living." But

I did not find any other objectionable thing against the teacher, barring that episode, hence I stopped myself from doing that. Till now, I remember the incident but have not discussed with her about it while we have done many programs thereafter. I observed she is becoming more considerate in her later interactions with participants. I think, everyone has his/her own learning graph and perhaps, that was her first brush with practical aspect discipline while she was still learning, hence it looked ugly to some of us.

Undoubtedly, I benefitted immensely from the program, the "Sudarshan Kriya" taught in the program was highly effective. Till date, I practice different exercises along with "Sudarshan Kriya" on daily basis. Once I realized that the workshop was beneficial, I arranged same for many people including my immediate relatives and neighbours. I encouraged many of my friends to get benefitted from the program. One thing, I have noticed that faith and discipline play a key role in effectiveness of this type of processes. If one does not have faith in the process, then it will leave little impact on him and if one does not follow it with certain regularity, then also, the effect will be very miniscule.

Amidst all these activities, I was reading the booked gifted by my friend about which I already have mentioned. The book was written by Sadhguru. There, he has described about the simple process called "Isha Kriya." I downloaded the video from the internet and started practicing it. I replaced the chanting of "Mahamrityunjaya mantra" with Isha kriya. It did not notice much difference, but the concept was very different and attractive, hence I continued the practise of Isha kriya regularly. Even now I practise that, sometimes, as a type of meditation process.

Now a days, my daily yoga session is maintained in a punctual way. On those days, when I am totally out of time, I will plan for minimum of five minutes in the morning to do the "Sudarshan Kriya" before the breakfast. These five minutes are the bare minimum, I rarely miss that. "Sudarshan Kriya" is an unavoidable daily routine for me. If I can squeeze out 20-30 minutes in the morning, then I complete the total process including the

"Sudarshan Kriya". I extend my session to one and half hours when I have plenty of time for myself. Apart from my health regime, my hands are always full, doing something or other till I lie down on my bed in the night.

V
Marriage on Cards

My mom was really concerned for my marriage. She wanted me to get married as soon as possible. My younger sister and elder brother had got married long time back and they have added new members to their families long ago. Hence, it was my turn, and the marriage was getting delayed for so many reasons.

About my health, she was worried, but she was in the believe that I would be healthy soon. She thought that if I could get consultations of good doctors, I would be able get rid of my problems. As a caring mother, she wanted to ensure that I got married to a good and 'cultured' girl. There were so many conditions laid down by her, it was just impossible for me, and to all of our relatives, to find someone matching to those criterions.

Luckily, things fell in place, and I got engaged to my one and only wife by the end of year 2012. Those are different story and will not fit into the theme of this book; I may need to write another for that purpose.

As I was getting closer to be a married man, I was realizing the importance of marriage in life. As I was going through the wonderful days approaching marriage, a kind of new thought had occurred to my mind. I began believing that being a couple helps in increasing survival chances of both. I did not have found any data supporting that thought but logically, it makes sense. Relationship and staying closer leads to some kind of solidarity among the couple and thus, provided everything is normal between them, it becomes advantageous for them to face the challenges life throws upon each human being. I am sure, this cannot be universally true. Relationship, especially, between a man and a woman, as a couple, in these days has become overly complex and they find it tough to navigate and ends up unexpectedly in a very disastrous way. I will not go much deep into this as many words have been said and many books have been written on this topic, but I could not stop myself from narrating a small but immensely powerful (to me) show in a documentary video.

I was watching a documentary show in one of the popular wildlife channels. It was wildlife survival demonstration by a survival expert. He is one of my favourites, till date. He is described as retired agent of British special forces and have done series of wildlife survival episodes in the TV. So, coming back to the show, in that day, he was presented as thirsty and hungry after days of toiling through the dense wild vegetation, in a semi-starved condition. He was surviving days in the harsh jungle, as depicted in the show, by eating flesh of small preys or insects or any eatable vegetation. Snake was, as he had declared, for him a full meal due its size. At a point of time, he came face to face with a medium sized snake, most probably a non-poisonous snake. He was happy to see the snake as he could kill it for his hungry stomach. He was about the catch and kill the snake but abandoned the idea of killing it after he saw its mate following it. The two snakes were a couple as per him and he could see love happening between them. That made him shelve his idea of consuming any of the two snakes, even he was hungry and needed food.

I related this story to my own self. I thought that my mom might be advising the right step. Having a partner in life will double the chances of survival. Probably many of our enemies, like, the survival expert, may give up the idea of killing us or we will be able face with dual force. Although these are light-hearted thoughts, but our mythologies and histories are ripe with this kind of motivating stories. One of the popular Indian mythological stories is the story of Savitri and Yamraj (Indian mythological king of death). As the story goes, Savitri, wife of Satyavan, followed and argued with Yamraj to get back the life of her husband, which he (Yamraj) was taking away. Due to her intelligence and never-ending love for her husband, she was able to convince Yamraj and make him (Satyavan) alive again.

I have witnessed myself that in the time of grief and despair, a little bit of positive thought or positive attitude helps a lot to overcome those challenging times. A positive thought or a positive step can change the destiny of life and an individual with positive attitude can change the fate of his group. Till date, I passionately believe in it.

Marriage happened in the year 2013, but that was not to come so easily. I have already mentioned that my mom and maternal uncles were followers of certain religious group. As per tradition, they used to go to the head of that group and took blessings from him before initiating any major activity. Hence, for my marriage too, they wanted to take me for his blessings. Reluctantly, I agreed and arranged travel plan for few of us (my uncle and few others). As the place, where we were supposed to meet him (head of the group), was outside Assam, we took train route to reach the place. I am refraining from mentioning any name and place to avoid any sort of controversy.

The journey began as we planned. We reached there in twenty-four hours of journey, checked into a hotel close to the 'Ashram' (residential area where the head and family resides) and went on to do an introductory visit. I had never visited any Ashram prior to that and in my imagination, as per mythological stories, Ashram was like few cottages in middle of forest where Guru would teach his disciples in peaceful and serene environment. The ashram we were visiting did not matched to my imagination. The buildings were impressive and well-developed. The campus was quite large, and I could see quite substantial number of permanent residents were there inside the campus. It had its own small hospital and pharmacy. The Ashram also had its own formulations of herbal medicines. The Ashram was self-sufficient in the sense that they had everything inside the campus to meet the basic human needs.

Next day, we went on to visit the head of the group. He was descendant of the founder and final authority for the followers. Meeting him was not easy. You can see him from distance, but his attendants would not allow everyone get closer and meet him. He was sitting in the dais, and his devotees were seating on the carpet laid over ground inside a temporary tent of generous size. He was not throwing any sermon or talk and most of the time all were sitting silent except some discussions between him and his attendants. We too went there, and my uncle whispered to my ears, "Sit within direct view of him (head of the Group), his view also has miraculous effect on us."

I was not too convinced but there was no point of argument at that moment. So, I tried my best to not to argue but follow his instructions diligently. I saw that most of the 'devotees' would come and prostrate in front of him and would deposit some amount in the box, which was kept on the carpet, in front of the people sitting there. Thereafter they would sit on the carpet laid in front area of him. The senior devotees were sitting closer to him, and other general devotees were sitting beyond a nominal barricading. (The sect follows a ranking among the devotees depending on the commitment and capability. They offer certain preacher positions to some sincere devotees and those preachers are held in high regard among the sect).

On that day, I noticed some were bringing few fruits, which were probably grown at their home and offering to the 'Head.' The head told to one of them that he could not eat them, but he (devotee) could give those to other family members. I was thinking to myself, "Yes, devotion has the power, and it works both ways. Its beneficial to both devotee and the worshipped. Devotee gets benefitted out of his devotion and the worshipped gets his due share."

Nothing happened on the Second day, as my uncle could not 'arrange' a meeting with the head of group. My uncle wanted to discuss about my health along with blessings for the marriage. On third day, things were becoming urgent as we were supposed to leave on fourth night. We could not wait there for an extra day as all our tickets were booked and no tickets could be booked in short notice. If we were unable to meet the 'head' on third day, then chances of getting an appointment will reduce and purpose of whole journey will be nullified. I was also interested as my uncle had insisted that he (the head) had the knowledge and power to end my sufferings.

Things were not different on third day too. The attendants were not allowing the devotees to speak to the head except 'darshan' from distance. We were told that he was not keeping good health. But I saw few groups of people would have audience with him. I said to uncle to approach him directly, instead of waiting further. I was suggesting to him repeatedly. But he lacked courage to do so.
Hence, I told him, "Should I myself approach and try to discuss?"

He took kind of sigh of relief and told me, "Yes, you can go directly. You can speak the local language, right?"

I nodded and gathered my courage to approach the head.

I did customary prostrating and deposited five hundred rupees (voluntarily), put in an envelope, to the wooden box kept in front of him and proceeded closer to him to seek his resolution to my problems. I was about to say something to him (the head) but one of his attendants caught hold of me and asked me why I am going closer to him. I told him I need to discuss my problems like stomach ailment and other issues with the head. He retorted in an insulting voice, "And you think that he (the head) will be able to relieve of your stomach pain?"

I was stumped by his question. Indeed, I was beginning to believe that the head would show me some way even he did not have any magical wand. I looked surprisingly to him. He shoved me aside by saying, "Please don't bother him now!"

I returned to where my uncle was sitting and told him what all happened. He was also seeing all the happenings, so he had nothing to say.

Later, we stood in a que to get audience with the son of the head, who was sort of second in command. He spoke to me and suggested to visit one of the doctors there in the campus. I went to the doctor and the doctor, after seeing my medical history, suggested, as expected, to continue same medication. We returned the other day and my experience with the Ashram ended there.

I discussed the same incidents with my younger brother, who said some logical words to me at that moment, which still I find lot fascinating. "Bother, I have figured out that in our country of vast population, large chunk people who does not have access to quality healthcare and other civic facilities, have firm believe in their minds that their troubles can be solved by some Godman", he said to me in a consoling tone.

I understand what he said is true and that is because, in our Indian culture some of the Gurus are proven to be incredibly wise and held in extremely high regard. The tradition of "Guru-Shishya Parampara" (Traditions of Master and disciple) is continuing in this country from the time immemorial and we all are proud of it. Great chunk of population still believes in this age-old tradition, and they approach them (Gurus) for advice and guidance. This is very normal in our land, and many are benefitted. But the imposters are bringing bad name to the tradition. Thus, my search for a true Guru was not yet accomplished. Oh yes, the blessings for my marriage were obtained from the "second in command" only.

Spirituality has deeply influenced me throughout my life. Since my childhood, I used to debate with others on the topic of existence of God, correctness of various religious process, characteristics of the religious groups among Hinduism and other religions. I used to debate about vegetarian and non-vegetarian food habits, about believers and non-believers of idol worship and many other topics related to religion and God. There were many doubts in mind which I used to discuss with elders, sometimes I was satisfied, sometimes their answers did not seem reasonable to me at that point of time. Sometimes, some of behaviours or concepts impressed me a lot. This way, unknowingly, a principled belief system was shaping up inside me since childhood.

One instance in my childhood caused lot of confusion in my mind. My native place was a village, but it was multicultural neighbourhood. There were, and even now also, many communities living together at the same area. Among the tribes, Karbi, Dimasa, Bodo, Tiwa, Garo etc. and among other communities Assamese, Bengali, Bihari, all were living peacefully in that area for decades. Few families of Sikhs & Christians were also there in our place. There was a small marketplace, were we used to visit for all our needs. One of the monthly routines was the haircut. I used to go to a barber shop. There in that shop, I could see a poster of 'Baba' with grey hair and beard, sitting comfortably in his 'asana' (yogic posture). (Normally 'Baba' is a respectable term for a man with wisdom, in some Indian language father is also called as 'Baba' by his offsprings)

The poster was there for many years, and I saw that poster in many other places too. When I become capable enough to read the vernacular literature, I could realize that at the bottom of the poster few lines are written in local scripts, which I will, in my limited capacity, translate to English, as "In thick of forest, in the middle of battle, in the depth of water, wherever you are; Just think about me, I will save you."

These few sentences caused lot of turbulence in my young impressionable mind. At that stage, I had that simple notion that if something was written, then it had to be true. The textbooks, the newspapers, the religious scriptures all were true, otherwise someone would object and would make that right. Since, that poster made such tall claim of saving anyone who is in trouble, just by mere remembrance; I was thinking, "Can this be possible? Will a tiger shy away from me in jungle if I remember about that Baba? Will a soldier be spared by his opponent in the battlefield if he prays to the Baba in his mind?"

Since, my childhood these questions bothered me a lot and many seniors whom I consulted did not have any concrete answer. This was stored as an unanswered question from my memory from

Childhood.

Few years back when I heard a similar statement from another Babaji, the flashback of the childhood question came to my mind. Now, I started thinking again and without any presumptions or bias. After few days, I could understand that the efficacy of the statement made by the Baba is cent percent.

Surprised?

Yes, I was also surprised when this logic came to my mind. The concept was simple. Suppose a person is inside a dense forest and due to his sheer bad luck, he comes across a ferocious lion. Then, there is only two possibilities, either the person will survive to tell the story, or he will be a meal of the lion. Let us assume that he remembered the Baba when he had come across the lion and was able to escape with some significant injury or little injury. Now, he will live rest of his life to tell the story about his escape from lion in the jungle and how miraculous Baba's remembrance is. He will tell this to every interested person and possibly he will dedicate his life to the Baba.

On the other side of the story, if the person was not able to escape the lion and had become its (lion's) meal; nobody will be able to know whether he had remembered Baba or Kaaba. But the Baba's follower will claim that the dead person did not remember Baba's name and hence the lion killed him. Like the saying, "There is no one, reporting parachute failure!"

Thus, after so many years, I found the answer to my childhood question. The message on the poster hanged on the wall of a barber shop in my village was hundred percent effective. Only survivors will narrate how Baba's remembrance helped him/her to escape death.

Lot of stuffs happened during the days of marriage. Marriage, in our culture is not less than a month-long affair because it leads you to an affair of seven births, it is another matter whether one believes in it or not! So, stories and memories are inevitable. But few of my memories are funny and never happened in my life types. As I have already mentioned, that during my marriage, I was not totally fit and just recovering from my illness, these incidents gave me some moments of distraction from my routine frustrating thoughts on my illness and to some extent as a source of motivation to trudge ahead.

It is customary, in our culture, for the groom to spend the immediate night at in-law's place post solemnization of marriage. As per custom, the bride is separated from the groom, after all the marriage ceremony is complete for the evening, until her hand is handed to him again next morning, when everyone is ready to start journey to groom's place. That is the time bride, and her family members get emotional and some kind of sombre atmosphere is created at bride's place. Some of the family members of accompany her to groom's place. There are stories, which tell that, earlier the groom had to stay at in laws place for months. His capabilities to start and run a family in assessed by in-laws in those days. They would set up various test methods and would give him difficult assignments during that period. They will hand over their daughter to him only if they are satisfied that he can shoulder the responsibilities.

For me, luckily, it was just a night and there was no test set me for. Had there been any test, chances were high, given my health, that I would have to return empty handed.

Thus, in the first morning after my marriage was solemnized, I got up early from the bed to get ready to return home. I awoke my best man, who too had stayed with me at my in laws place for the night. Next thing I did was to lookout for my laptop bag, where I had kept all my bathroom kit and some bare essential items like comb, few garments, card purse and wallet with some currency notes. I also had kept my second mobile handset along with charger in that bag, but the laptop was not in that bag as I had purposefully left that at my home.

I remembered that I had kept that just beside the bed in the room where both of us (me and my best man) were sleeping and the door had been locked properly. I searched nook and corner of the room but could not find the bag. My best man too had no clue. I moved out of the room to ask if someone had moved it. Within few minutes, everyone was asked, and every room was searched but the bag was nowhere to be found. Everyone present there admitted of seeing it coz I was handling it myself fearing that it may get lost. My best man was carrying it all the time and I remembered having it till going to bed.

All become concerned and started checking out various possibilities. One of my in-law's family members told us that he had seen a boy walking out with a bag when he opened the main gate of the residence. He even had enquired the boy about the bag. The boy had replied to him that he was with the cameraman (the videographer, who was covering the marriage ceremony for the whole night), and the bag belonged to the cameraman. Convinced with reply, he had allowed the boy to get away with the bag. Immediately the cameraman was enquired, and he informed that he did not ask anyone to carry his bag, and his bag was with him.

Then it became clear that the bag was stolen by the boy. When all this discussion was going on, my other handset (less expensive, without camera) started ringing non-stop. I was getting one call after another. First was my brother asking me how my land purchase agreement got its place in dustbin at Hojai railway station. I had no clue to his queries. I thought, "I am already in big trouble. Now, what is this again. Who had taken my land agreement documents and placed them in a dustbin at the railway station?"

Second call was from my maternal uncle (who had taken me to the Ashram), and remaining calls were from my friends. By the third call I learned that the boy, rather a kid, who had stolen my bag, had been apprehended at Hojai railway station by GRP (Government Railway Police) team.

I was taken aback. I thought, "So fast! how can one lose and get back the items so easily?"

It took few moments to let the feeling sink in.

I got all my items back next day along with all the items and most importantly currency notes from the Hojai Police station. I did not know how much amount was inside the bag, I got back few thousands, and I did not care. I was extremely happy and feeling blessed divinely to get back my all of my items inside the bag. Now, I must keep my readers happy by narrating what happened beyond my eyes, otherwise the curiosity will remain with them forever.

The boy, after being able to get away from my in-law's place, rushed to Hojai Railway station, probably to escape to Guwahati with those items. Perhaps, he was waiting for train at the railway station along with other passengers. In those days, few passengers used to turn up for early morning trains. The boy, while waiting for the train, was checking out the materials inside the bag, may out of his own curiosity to know how good his hand was. He was throwing away those items which he thought of no value. He threw aways items like paper, slips etc.

His activity caught attention of the two of persons present in the station. One of them was my in-laws neighbour who had a tea-stall in that station. Other one was cousin brother of one of my close friends. They suspected, thanks to their alert mind, something amiss. An expensive mobile taken out from that bag, Currency notes were taken out and counted, some items were discarded – they were watching all these activities of the kid. They got suspicious and collected one piece of paper the boy had thrown away. To my sheer luck, it was my land purchase document, which I had kept in a pocket inside the bag and have forgotten about it.

They read out my name from the bag. The in-law's neighbour immediately recognized, and said to the other person, "This name matches with the name of groom of the wedding last night in our neighbourhood. I have seen the name in the invitation card. I am sure this boy had stolen the bag from the place of marriage ceremony last night."

My friend's cousin too recognized the name and said to him," Yes, I think so. Let us catch him and get hold of the bag."

"Wait, I have better idea. I will keep a watch on him and you, please, go and call the GRP." My in-laws neighbour whispered to him.

Things happened as both planned and rest of the sequence of events, which led to the items reaching its original owner, can easily be imagined.

I had profusely thanked both gentlemen for their alertness and presence of mind which helped me to get back my items without an iota of hardship on my part. I even offered them gifts in return, but both declined to it.

Now, when I recollect the incident, two thoughts criss-cross my mind. One, how important for us to remain alert and vigilant to stop any crime from happening and the other, probable grime outlook for the child's future. After being caught perhaps in his maiden attempt, the child, if corrective measures were not taken, would have become highly proficient thief or criminal by learning from his mistakes. Second part is the greatest tragedy getting repeated with small time criminals becoming full time criminals who do not shy away from committing heinous crimes.

VI

The final assault

After marriage, our first trip together was to Bengaluru. We stayed few days at city and at the Art of Living Ashram Bengaluru. There we attended 5 days Advance Meditation course, physically attended he Satsang (religious discourse) of Sri Sri Ravishankar, the founder of Art of Living society and took his blessings. We roamed around Bengaluru and returned home. Till then my physical condition was nowhere near normal but somehow, I was managing the things. The strategy employed by me in those days was like neither to make me lethargic by sitting idle nor to indulge too much. I kept my difficulties to myself and told others that I am on the path to recovery. I was also trying my best to get rid of my troubles and there was firm believe deep in my heart that I will be able to overcome my illness.

My better half still laments that our first trip post marriage was to an Ashram. But that was the need of the hour. In Hindi language, there is a saying, which says, "*Jaan he to Jahan he,*" which translates to "World exists till you are alive." I try to make her understand that I had made that choice coz I want to keep her happy for rest of her life.

Almost a year after my marriage, most probably towards the end of year 2015, my wrist pain flared up and I never know that this pain would lead me to entirely different things. It happened for certain reason for which I must blame myself. One of my cousin sisters was suffering from the most dreaded disease, which we call cancer, for a year. She took her last breath someday in the last months of 2015. She died in the evening and her funeral happened the next day in the morning. I had stayed awake whole night along with few others to guard the body of my late cousin sister and worked for the arrangement of her funeral next morning. I lifted few heavy woods to arrange her funeral pyre and returned home for rest after completion of the process.

Next morning, when I woke up, found my wrist paining unbearably. There was burning sensation around the wrist, and it was becoming difficult even to move my fingers. I felt the intense heat and pain and I was sure that one of my old 'friends' is visiting me again. At that point of time, I was not having any medication for my rheumatoid arthritis and was relying on yoga and food control. I realized that due to my previous day's strain on my body by keeping myself awake whole night and lifting heavy weight by my hands, this condition had arisen. I have observed that in rheumatoid arthritis, any minor cause can lead to a very aggravated condition of the disease and the patient ends up in a very miserable condition from otherwise manageable condition. In my case also, same thing happened. I was somehow managing with little bit of pain on my left wrist, and I was happy with that, as I knew that rheumatoid arthritis is not a curable disease. But, in this aggravated condition, I knew that merely yoga a food regime will not be able to reduce my suffering; I would have to visit a consultant for my situation.

The pain become awfully sustaining. The pain will be intense in the morning and evening. My wife and my mom became very much worried, and they tried to help me by massaging with several types of oils. But nothing was helping me, and I wanted to cry at my helpless situation. Those last two to three years, the wrist pain was there but it was becoming bearable to me as it did not aggravate. I did not want to go back to the harmful allopathic medicines for RA; hence, I went to local Homoeopathic doctor, who was practising since my childhood. He assured me that the pain will go away soon.

I took his medicines and few liquids, which he had given for external application as pain reliever. I continued his treatment for almost 10 to 15 days. But, instead of getting healed my wrist swelled to its double

size and pain was tremendous.

It occurred to me that it is better to die by side effects of allopathic medicines instead of dying in bits with pain. I went to Guwahati and visited the best rheumatologist. It was difficult to get his appointment, but somehow, I could get his appointment. I explained full story to him straight from beginning, he also did few confirmatory blood tests. He dropped my mainstay drug, i.e., Pentasa, and advised a drug which will work both for RA as well as Crohn's disease. With great apprehension, I asked him whether those drugs contained steroid. He replied that without steroid it was not possible to contain my problem. I was devasted! but still not willing to give up the fight. I came out from his cabin with my prescription in hand.

While I was going to buy the medicines, my elder brother called me up. He was worried about my health as he knew very well about it. He stayed as an attendant several times with me in the hospitals in Mumbai. He passed on an information to me that there was a good Homoeopathic doctor in Guwahati. He told me to try it as he himself was cured of his eye problem under the homoeopathic doctor's treatment.

I had already two encounters with two homoeopathic doctors and results were not very much encouraging to give a third try. But I changed my mind when he (my elder brother) told me that before coming to the homoeopath, for his eye disease, the ophthalmologists in Mumbai had recommended surgery as only cure with 50% chance of recovery. The homoeopathic doctor, whom he was referring, cured his eye condition with simple homoeopathic medicines. This part of information made me rush to the doctor.

I already had bought a bagful of allopathic medicine as per the prescription by the rheumatologist. From the pharmacy, I took the straight drive to the Homoeopath's chamber. The consultations were through prior appointments there was no free slot for the day. I requested them and showed the condition of my wrist. They gave me the last appointment in the evening. I waited from 4 O'clock to 9 O'clock in that evening for my consultation.

His name is Dr. Dhruba Jyoti Biswas, a pass out from a reputed Homoeopathic college in state of Karnataka- still practising successfully in Guwahati, Assam. His approach was professional. He gave me a patient hearing, checked all the reports, and commented that he could not cure my problem but could reduce the pain by 80%. At that moment even if he had said 50%, I would have gleefully accepted his treatment. I thought if I get cured of 80%, then I can manage the rest very easily through Yoga and proper diet plan. I was telling myself that I would be satisfied if he could bring my health back to the condition it was few weeks earlier. He advised some diet restrictions and told me to reduce the intake of allopathic medicines in gradual manner to stop completely by a month, as the Homoeopathic medicines, as per him, would take almost a month to show its effect.

For the first time in my life, I saw a homoeopathic doctor writing prescription. He wrote down his findings from the test reports, advised medicines and recommended some investigations on his letterhead and passed on the slips to his assistants for packing the medicines for me. I was feeling like, "Wow! he writes prescription too!" During the consultation, he pointed out that my Anti-CCP test result level was around seventy-five. He told me that my pain would reduce as the level should come down post medication.

His professional approach impressed me quite a lot. I realized that I had never consulted with a fully trained doctor of Homoeopathic stream. All those Homoeopathic doctors I have interacted till date, I believe, were self-trained by reading few books at home. I also discussed with him about my stomach ailment and haemoglobin deficiency disease. He told me that he would first give medicines for RA and Chron's disease and will see other issues later. Finally, after long wait, I walked out of the Homoeopathic centre burdened with confusing thoughts and two bags of medicine on my hand, one homoeopathic and other allopathic.

I started taking his medications, stopped all the allopathic medicines within a month except few vitamins for my haemoglobin deficiency. The medicines were working, and my spirit lifted many folds- I felt like a bird released from its cage and ready to fly high. The mere joy of getting rid of the allopathic medicines at that stage was immense. I felt like a big burden had been removed from my head; I felt livelier! When I was having those steroid based and NSAID allopathic drugs I know that those were harmful for my body but still I could not avoid them as those helped me manage my medical condition. Now with joy of getting rid of those medicines and managing with some harmless looking homeopathic liquid bottles took me to cloud number nine.

The treatment and follow up continued. My endless debate with Dr. Himamoni Deka, (a childhood friend and Assistant Professor at Guwahati Medical College) about efficiency of various stream of treatment continued. My arguments got more emboldened with my improvement in health using Homoeopathic medicines.

In those days, a kind of sarcastic incident happened. My treatment was progressing by timely visits to the clinic of the Homoeopathic doctor; in one of the visits, he advised me to bring a whole abdomen ultrasound scan. As per suggestion of Dr. Himamoni, I visited one of reputed radiologist at Bhangagarh in Guwahati. While doing the investigations, he asked me about my complications. I told him, "I have Crohn's disease, I have Rheumatoid Arthritis, I have Haemoglobin E-disease, I have ......" Before I could complete the list, he interrupted, "Stop, Stop... That is enough...You are living with so much of troubles... I do not dare to listen anymore."

I was amused at his reaction. I saw for the first time a doctor reacting that way. After a pause, he asked me again, "So, what are you doing to get rid of these difficulties?"

I thought I must answer this question. "Homoeopathic treatment in Guwahati" I said calmly.

"What?" He sounded astonished, "Are you kidding me? Why don't you go to a good hospital and consult good doctors?"

"Sir, I have visited all the good hospitals and consulted all the good doctors starting from Guwahati to Mumbai and up to Delhi," I gave him my readymade answer.

After hearing me he thought for some time and advised me, "Then you can go for better hospitals abroad."

I was laying down on the bed while we conversed. I just gave him a blank look and said nothing. He too said nothing and completed the procedure. He too must also have realized that going abroad for treatment is not a joke. Enormous funds requirement will be the biggest challenge and on top of that getting proper treatment and consultation there when you will be going for the first time will not be an easy thing. While I walked out of his chamber, I thought that I would come back to him with my reports if I happened to get recovered through the Homoeopathic treatment.

Yoga, homeopathic medicines, food control and time management worked like a miraculous formula. I thought I was able to reverse back from the turning point, I marked for myself, in the year 2011, when I had dreamt of being lowered into a grave. My performance improved, my weakness was gone, and I felt like I had come to level playing field with my friends and colleague. During the recovery period, I recollect, there were many days, when a particular thought would suddenly crop up in my mind, "Today is the best day in my life; I never found myself this much fit!"

I started to fit myself slowly to the real world. I began re-testing my limits. First, I focused on my physical strength, like how long I could walk; for short and medium distances, I would walk, or I would use public transport like shared auto, bus, train etc. for long distance travels. I checked how long I can work continuously without break. I compared myself with younger generations working on the same job. My confidence re-established when I could see myself matching up with them. I also indulged myself in sports like badminton. All those indicated me gaining in health and strength.

I restarted my pet projects in various fields. I was very much interested in cultivation. I focused on banana plantation and learned various nuances of the process. Starting from the plantation to ripening of the final product, I become very much involved with the entire process. Even though it was in small scale, it gave me lots of satisfaction. Investment and trade were another field of my interests; I started focusing on that part too and started a consulting business with few employees. All these started with my recovery process. I realized that the recovery process is like growing a tree. Once a plant grows to a big tree, all the branches, leaves, fruits everything comes on its own. We do not need to add anything to it, apart from nourishing its roots; the complete process is organic.

In work front, my focus increased, and my co-workers and superiors were happier with my contribution. My performance evaluation rating increased from initial years at offshore. I too felt that I could become more involved in the tasks at offshore. I took some initiative at workplace to bridge a healthy working relationship with all other departments working at offshore. All these started showing results and I become very much inspired. In those days, I got the opportunity of associating myself with the development of Vivekananda Kendra Vidyalaya, Tumpreng, a non-profit CBSE 10+2 school, managed by Vivekananda Kendra Siksha Prachar Vibhag, which in turn is a part of Vivekananda Rock Memorial and Vivekananda Kendra Trust based at Kanyakumari, Tamil Nadu. I was present in the very first meeting. I got involved in the process from the initial stage. I collected donations from all my friends and colleagues. We conducted lottery for school fund. Went to various govt departments and ministries for help and support.

As in this year 2021, when I am writing this piece, it gives me immense pleasure that the RCC construction of 15000 sqft is completed another five thousand sqft construction is under progress. The project is far away from completion but whatever has been done till date is remarkable.

On family front, we as a couple, had spent lakhs of rupees on various fertility treatments as there was some issue with us. I learnt many terms like, IVF, ICSI during the treatment process. We had undergone various tests and processes at a reputed hospital in Guwahati. The fertility expert in the hospital did two rounds of implantation of embryo for lakhs of rupees for each of the rounds. But results of both the tests were negative. My wife had to undergo physical suffering with every round but the emotional suffering with negative results at the end was highly devastating.

Not seeing any results from abroad groomed fertility expert, we thought of discussing the issue with our Karnataka educated Homoeopathic physician. Our other family members were also suggesting for homoeopathic treatment. Both of us went to him and discussed the issue. All the test report were available with us already. He saw those reports and advised some medications. Magic! Within few months we got the result and after one year we become proud parent of a healthy baby.

Allopathic or Homoeopathic comparison is not a part of my writings in this piece, but should there not be a mechanism in place, which helps individuals to choose and follow the procedure which has more effectiveness? Take the example of modern techniques like IVF and ICSI. This process must be unavoidable for someone; but does every childless couple need those costly processes. Like in my case, many may get better result by following other treatment process like Homoeopathy. And what is the success rate of the IVF, ICSI? The fertility expert had told me its 50%. But we had done two rounds, but results are negative in both rounds. Then, the success rate does not remain 50%.

When I went first time to that hospital, where we did our fertility procedures, I saw a photo of a baby was pasted on the notice board of the hospital as a successful story of the IVF process. My heart sunk, seeing the image. I thought that being a fertility centre it should have displayed the number of successful couples who had gone there for treatment. But, again, I was not aware of other options at that point of time. But now, I feel sympathy for many gullible childless couple, like us, wasting lakhs of their hard-earned money and precious time before attempting other cheaper, effective, and more organic options.

As a sufferer and conqueror of my diseases like Crohn's, Arthritis, Impotency, and many others. I feel sympathetic with so many patients, whom I had seen in long waiting queues for the consultation outside the doctors' chambers, when I was also like one of them. I knew none of them, do not know how they are faring in their life now, do not have any idea about their struggles with their diseases. If I meet anyone suffering like I suffered in my earlier period of life, I share them my story and show them the best way forward.

During the peak of my suffering, I was taking lots of medicines as suggested by so many allopathic consultants, I was visiting. There were 10-15 tablets and capsules consumed by me on daily basis. Seeing me doing that, my youngest maternal uncle would mock me, "You will not die of disease but of the medicines. Why do you need to take so many tablets?"

The disease was killing me from inside and on top of that hearing such remarks made me lose all my controls, "Okay, I will stop taking all these medicines, which I am taking as per advice of medical experts. Now, you give me the alternative treatment.," I would yell to his face, "Can you?"

Now, I realize that the opinion and advise of the experts have their own value, but everyone is susceptible to human error and amid so many experts and opinions, the chance of unintentional error and communication gap widens. Hence, one must take second opinion before committing with some procedure or treatment regime. It is good development that now a days people are becoming more informed about treatment options like Homoeopathic, Ayurvedic, Yogic Practices. Many people like me have experienced healing powers of these alternative streams and have benefitted themselves immensely.

VII
Feeling being at Zenith

A journey does not end, and it continues. Life, death, pain, comfort all these are part of this 'endless' journey. Nobody, till date, has attempted to prove that time travels in circular path. Till date the path of time is accepted as straight and non-repetitive. We all are travellers unaware of our destination and more confusingly doubtful of existence of even the "final destination." In all our thought and action our consciousness plays a significant role and again while attempting to understand the consciousness leads us to something called supreme consciousness. Many enlightened souls have tried to explain supreme consciousness and bring it to masses on their own way of presentation. But again, getting it from someone else's experience and taking it first-hand it quite different. For firsthand experience, first, we need to become enlightened!

Journey will be endless, but a piece writing must stop somewhere. I have narrated my entire journey of those special periods of my life and few incidents which I will not forget for whole of my life. I would like end by telling you how I feel now, i.e., 2021, after ten years of peak of my illness. I have stopped taking all kinds of medicine after taking Homoeopathic medicines from the same doctor for three years. In those years, I religiously followed all the medicine regimes and doctor's instructions along with my daily dose of yoga, meditation, and diet control. Now, I occasionally take few multivitamins and calcium. I do regular PME and fortunately all reports indicate good health. Now, I can walk, jump, run, swim and can do whatever I wish. I can work 18 hours at a stretch without any major break. I have tested it many occasions at home or office. I do not have problem with sleep anymore; I sleep like dead person when I lie down for sleep at around 10:00 PM. I must mention that now I am able to ride bicycle and motorcycle effortlessly, which was impossible for me few years earlier because of my arthritic left wrist. (I never gave up car driving as it is a single-handed affair for me.). At the age of 43 years, I feel at my the fittest best and I am ready to test my limits anytime.

In search of my health, now I feel that I have reached a place, for which I was praying to God immensely to take me to, when I was suffering from the worst of health condition of my life. This way this is a great victory for me, and I celebrate the gift of God everyday with total dedication towards my work and health.

Some of the health regime, I follow, I thought, you may be interested:

1. I say good night to everyone by 10:30 PM every night, if there is no emergency.

2. I do not sleep in daytime. If I feel sleepy, I just sit on a comfortable chair and rest for some
time. But I do not lay down my back on a flat surface in daytime.

3. I do not oversleep; I sit-up on my bed as soon as I am awake, may it be winter or summer.

4. Normally, I take two times meal with little bit of snack in the noontime.

5. I prefer vegetarian dishes. Among non-veg, I take egg or local Sweetwater fish only.

6. I do not take heavy meal or non-veg meal post sunset.

7. I prefer to take dinner by 8:30 PM.

8. I brush my teeth only once, after dinner before going to bed. In the morning, I gurgle with lukewarm salted water.

9. I drink lots of water, around four litres every day. I drink at least a litre of lukewarm water in the morning.

10. I neither smoke nor drink alcoholic beverages, not even so-called soft drinks available in the market.

11. I occasionally take few vitamins and calcium as supplements.

12. Yoga, Meditation, and motivational talks are my favourite pastime.

13. I involve myself in all family, work, and social activities. As the Sadhguru (Jaggi Maharaj of Isha Foundation) had said in his commentaries, I feel the whole universe as my responsibility, but I choose to respond as per my capability and preference.

14. I dedicate a part of my work for the betterment of society around us.

I believe, every life is a journey of its own and during the journey one will have to face variety of phases. No point of lamenting or blaming anyone or self at any point of time. We just need to move from one phase to another. We like or not, there will be change. If we put our efforts wholeheartedly to guide it to desired direction, we will be successful to reach the goal.... Journey will continue....

With silent prayers to supreme consciousness, I wish all of you success in your own struggles.

VIII
Self-tried suggestions

Personally, I have faced lots of health issues and have recovered from them. In the process, I have learned tricks to prevent and recover from those. I am sharing few of my learnings with the caution note that something which is helpful may not be helpful for others and hence individual discretion is necessary.

Acidity: If one regularly suffering from acidity related troubles, then he must approach doctors for proper investigation and treatment. There can be several reasons for feeling of acidity like situation in stomach. There may be problem with gall bladder or excessive acid secretion or indigestion etc. Along with medical advice a little bit of tweak in eating habits works wonder. In condition of acidity following two are strongly recommended:

a. Drinking water in the morning while empty stomach.
b. Eating a bowl of roasted black chickpeas after removing its peel. It can be eaten anytime; best result is when eaten separately with a glass of water and not combining with other eatables.

Back pain: Swami Ramdeva recommends Markatyasana for this trouble. I have found this asana
highly effective. We should seek advice of the physiotherapy professional if we happen to develop back pain.

a. To prevent our back injury, we should focus on our sitting and standing postures. We should take care that our backbone remains in its natural erect position whether we are sleeping, sitting, or standing. If you take care of or backbone it will take care of your health for long
time.

b. Care should be taken while lifting weights. We should not bend our backs to lift any weight. Because we do not know how heavy something is until we try to lift it. Bending by waistline to lift a weight may result in immediate impairment of disks in the backbone. If you want to lift something then lower your height by bending your knees as much as you need, hold the item by your both hands and them attempt to lift it by straightening your knees.

c. Our sleeping mattress should not be too soft. Sleeping on soft mattresses leads to damage to the backbone.

d. One must take care while getting up from laying down posture of body. Just sitting up putting force on your back will aggravate your back pain. To do it in proper order, you take your left hand above your head, turn to left hand side, fold your right hand by elbow and now you rise laterally by putting force on both the hands.

Neck Pain (Spondylosis): This issue I will consider a lifestyle disease due to increasing number of populations using mobile phone or other interactive devices. For example, when we speak to someone over phone then we normally take the phone closer to ears or we use the headphone. But when we use the mobile phone or tablet for gaming, browsing or other interactive sessions, most of the people normally keep the phone on top the lap or just holds the phone with hands and looks down to it. Now, we all know that head is one of the heaviest parts of human body. When we will keep the head forward tilted for long duration the strain on the neck muscle and bone will be enormous and hence after some years this habit will make to go to doctor for treatment of your neck pain. To avoid it, you should hold the screen (of mobile, tablet, laptop) at the height equal to your eye position without bending your waist or neck.

Tennis Elbow: I learnt about this disease when the great Sachin Tendulkar was suffering. I learnt that this problem may arise due to our wrong habits with keyboard and mouse. The mouse/keyboard should be at same surface height with our elbow rest. Otherwise, our elbow may suffer from diseases like tennis elbow.

Insensitive finger skin: Touching the touchscreens with naked fingers should be avoided. Now a days most of the touchscreen devices come with stylus or touch pen. Originally, the touchscreens are not designed to be operated by fingers but with stylus. But with mass usages the use of fingers has become more prominent. But too much fingering of touchscreens may lead to damage in the foreskin of the fingers. Hence, best practice is to use the original pen/stylus.

Headache, Tiredness, muscle pain: Headache can have many causes, and it may require medical investigation if persisting for long time. Temporary headache, tiredness or muscle pain can be overcome by some simple tricks. When you face this any of this situation, first drink water if you are thirsty to ensure that your body is hydrated enough. Dehydration may lead to many unpleasant conditions including all three. If it is because of surrounding than try to change it if possible. Sit somewhere where is it comfortable for you. Keep your spine erect. Now, close your eyes and with count, do deep breathing; breath in for count 1 to 8 and breath out for count 9 to 16, allowing 1 second for each count. The breath in and breath out should be as slow as possible. You do it for 10 to 15 minutes, you will find yourself fresh again.

Sleeplessness: If the problem is very severe then medical consultation may be required. First one needs to ensure that he/she is not sleeping in the daytime. Somebody is sleeping hours in the daylight and complains about lack of sleep in the night. To get quality sleep at night, one should never sleep in daytime. Otherwise too, sleeping in daytime is not healthy; weakness, skeletal weakness, obesity, hormonal disorder all those may kick in.

There is one great technique to address sleeplessness and that is called – Meditation. Yes, meditate regularly for half an hour daily and you will see your sleeping process getting regularized. For beginners, you can split it into two sessions of 15 minutes each: one in the morning and keeping another for evening. Meditation should not be done post meal. Empty stomach condition is the best.

What if one gets up at odd hours in the night and not able to get back to sleep? Just sit back on bed with your spinal cord upright and start meditating. When you feel sleepy, then just lay back on your comfortable bed.

Meditation: I have mentioned so much for doing meditation, but how to do it? Nothing, just sit upright with your eyes closed. Yes, that is it! Isolate yourself into a comfortable room/corner of your home, get a yoga mat or something which insulates you from the floor but should not be too puffy then sit in any asana you are most comfortable with, bring your backbone to its natural posture, keep your hands on your laps, close your eyes, and there you go meditating! You should not meditate on your bed for so many reasons.

There are so many instructions available for doing meditation properly. But do not lose your head over those. Do not bother about thoughts or process during meditation or do not force anything as your thought. Just watch the different thoughts coming to your mind and accept them as they come. Do not react or open your eyes in between; if you open your eyes, then end your that session. Just sit like that as long as you feel like, and when you feel that you are done, lay down at same place (preferable) or on your bed without any pillow or head support. When you come back to your senses, you will feel like another fresh beginning for the day.

Yoga: Yoga is not only limited to asanas or breathing exercises; rather it is a living process. While you are walking or sitting, your walking & sitting posture should be as per yogic principle. Your behaviour and language should follow yogic principles. You can modify your eating habits as per yogic systems. Thus, you will find that yoga has addressed all spheres of human existence and behaviour. There are so many Yogic schools who conduct offline or online classes. You can enrol yourself into anyone and start your yogic journey. Initially, do not overstretch yourself and just try to follow their instructions. As I told you, it is a journey, a journey of Guru and Shishya, till the shishya can find himself at same level with Guru. Even though all Yogic schools teach yoga taught by Maharishi Patanjali, you may find some school's teaching not suiting to your personality. In that case, do not think much, just change your master until you find the one you are sync with. Here in India, as the story goes, Shishya goes out search for a perfect Guru and Guru too waits eagerly for a perfect disciple and when both meet magic happens. Arjun-Dronacharya, Chanakya-Chandragupta, Vivekananda-Ramkrishna Paramhansa, Ashoka-Guatam Buddha and the list does not end there.

Best Sleeping posture: The best sleeping posture for me is to sleep facing towards sky without any pillow, legs straight and both hands resting side by side. From digestion point of view sleeping on our left-hand side is recommended to be the best. Your left-hand side portion of body will be touching the bed, while the right hand will be folded by elbow to rest on palm on bed. You can alternate between the two postures if you find uncomfortable to sleep in a single posture.

Constipation: This is most common among people, and it is a morning blue for many people. If you are suffering from it and taking help of medicines, then stop worrying, you can get out of it without help of any medicine. You watch about your three habits,

   i. what you eat,
  ii. what you drink,
 iii. where you go.

So, following habits can be helpful:

a. Include fruits, leafy vegetables, and fibrous foods in your food basket. Change your biscuits to multigrain type, avoid meats and eggs for some days, go for fish instead, take whole fruits instead of juice. Banana is one of the best fruits and if you take orange, then just throw away the peels and seeds only, rest should go inside you. Cucumber is also another good option but should be taken during daytime. Take curd or buttermilk (chaas) instead of milk.

b. Reduce your liquids other than water; take plenty of water regularly, at least up to four litres on daily basis. Get hold of your water Jug after getting up from bed in the morning. Fill it with lukewarm water and keep on drinking from it slowly till the pressure builds up in your bladder or bowel. Initially, it will be difficult to take much water; hence start with a glass or two and later you can gradually step up it to one and half litre.

c. The type of your commode. For those who are suffering severely from irregular motion, I will suggest them to use Indian type of commode if they do not have difficulty otherwise. Squatting in Indian type of toilet, helps to push out the faeces out of your bowel. With these three habits you can cut down your laxative doses slowly and will be able to stop it completely to lead a normal life without medicines.

Antibiotics: This is my favourite topic. I discuss it among my colleagues and even with doctors when I get an opportunity. We guys need to be very much careful with antibiotics; one should never buy antibiotics over the counter and do self-medication. It should always be done under medical prescription and supervision. But I see the rampant abuse of antibiotics everywhere, be it in the city or at village, less people are aware about danger the antibiotics bring to them.

Let us discuss with an example. Suppose A has a developed fever on Monday morning, so he calls up his boss and asks for leave for the day, thinking that some rest will help him recover. His fever persists on Tuesday too, so he decides to visit a doctor, the doctor recommends some tests, but the tests results are all negative and hence the doctor tells him that he is just having viral fever.

Now, there are two types of doctors, some will send him away with some multivitamins and packets of ORS but some other will write antibiotics in his prescription. Now, till date, I have not come across a single medical professional who is able explain to me the reason of prescribing antibiotics for the treatment of viral fever. Some says that is to stop any secondary infection. Right, but where is the secondary infection. All reports are negative. "Are you going to tell me that you are using antibiotic as preventive medication?" I wonder at the intellect level of few doctors, "Does Antibiotics works like Titaneans injection."

Nobody has ever given me proper explanation, but some doctors still prescribe antibiotics to treat viral fever. Antibiotics by the name are anti-organism, they destroy human cells, beneficial bacteria as well as the harmful bacteria. They are like bombs, wherever they will explode damage will be multilateral. I was perfect two days earlier but under attack of virus now, my immune system is busy fighting with virus. The Virus are tough opponent as they can easily switch between living and non-living forms. Then you drop something into body which ineffective on the virus but brings down your immune system. You are helping your body or helping the virus?

In my family, when there is fever, and doctor confirms that it is a viral fever; I never allow anyone take antibiotic. His only treatment will be paracetamol and probiotic, good rest, and proper care. I have seen that after stopping haphazard use of antibiotics, people get back on their feet quicker in case of any kind of infections.

Another downside of using antibiotic without proper medical guidance is that if you stop taking the medicine without completing the recommended doses, then you are helping the bacteria strain. If you happen to sick next time with same type of bacteria strain, then you will have to use higher power dosages of antibiotics to get full recovery. This is because they(bacteria) mutate amazingly fast and develop defence mechanism against the partially administered antibiotic. If the mutated strain goes to another person, he too will have to take higher dose of antibiotic even that is the first case for him. Imagine, what will happen, if he too stops short of taking full dose of prescribed antibiotics. Its easy guess, the bacteria will mutate to a stronger version. This is what happening in India. Even the doctors are dying in TB hospitals due to MDR (Multi Drug Resistance) bacterial infections. The MDR strain of bacteria are like superbugs against which all types of existing antibiotics are ineffective. There was news reported that many foreign medical tourists dying in Indian super-speciality hospitals due to infection of these type of superbugs.

I feel horrified when I see people buying antibiotics over the counter on self-prescription and the pharmacists are too selling then for quick profit, flaunting all the guidelines. I got some relief, when I got the news that ICMR has issued strict guidelines for the medical practitioners to restrict and limit the use of antibiotics.

Loss or Gain weight: Interestingly, you want to either loss or gain weight, the process is same, if your target is to gain proper body weight as per your body structure. You need to focus again on three things,

i. Diet,
ii. Exercise, and
iii. Rest.

For diet, I have already explained, two times big meal; breakfast and early dinner is recommended with some light snacks or fruits for lunch. Water, Milk, Chas etc. should be taken in proper portion to keep body hydrated. Exercise is a must. Instead of hitting gym, it is better to practice yoga and meditation. Running and walking will also be helpful, but for running, the ground and shoes should be proper otherwise, you may damage your knee. I have already explained about rest. You should go to bed latest by 10:30 PM and wake up early morning after 6 to 7 hours sleep. Late night activity should be reduced, and day sleeping should be avoided. All these, if practiced in continuation will help in reducing weight. Thyroid is one key factor in weight gain/loss; hence one should consult doctors if the condition is alarming.

I have seen bulky individuals who is finds tough to move themselves due to their weight. One of my friends was a heavyweight (not a boxer!), he used to tell me, "Kya karoon yaar, mein agar paani bhi peeta hoon toh shareer me lag jata he!" (I am helpless friend, even if I drink plain water, my body adds in weight.)

"Yes dear, you are really in a tough situation," I sympathised with him, knowing that his office colleagues had complained to me that he had broken many wooden chairs sitting in the office!

One day, he invited me and another friend of mine for evening tea at his place. His better half brought us snacks and tea. I was amazed to see that he down gorged more than half of the snacks while we both watched. Then, only I came to understand that what is the "paani" he referred to.